AGS® *Reading Skills for Life*

Level D

AGS®

American Guidance Service, Inc.
Circle Pines, Minnesota 55014-1796
1-800-328-2560

Content Reviewers

The publisher wishes to thank the following educators for their helpful guidance and review during the development process for *Reading Skills for Life.* Their assistance has been invaluable.

Jack Cassidy, Ph.D.
Professor of Education
Texas A&M University
Corpus Christi, Texas

James Johnston
Reading Specialist
Portsmouth High School
Portsmouth, New Hampshire

Alva Webb Jones, Ed.S.
Special Education Consultant
Richmond County Board of Education
Augusta, Georgia

Robin Pence
Reading Specialist
Clay High School
Clay County Schools
Green Cove Springs, FL

Ted Stuff
School Psychologist
Special Education
    Department Chair
McLaughlin High School
Anchorage, Alaska

Development and editorial services provided by Inkwell Publishing Solutions, Inc.

Photo and Illustration Credits

Page 4, © Jeff Greenberg/PhotoEdit; p. 6, © David Young-Wolff/PhotoEdit; pp. 9, 12, 21, 41, 72, 79, 144, Wendy Cantor; p. 26, © Agence France Presse/Corbis; p. 34, © Galen Rowell/Corbis; p. 48, © PhotoDisc; pp. 55, 93, 107, © AP/Wide World Photos; pp. 67, 84, 128, 137, Aleksandra Remezova; p. 99, © Pat Rawlings/NASA HSF Gallery; p. 113, © Ecoscene/Corbis; p. 150, © Joe McDonald/Corbis; pp. 125, 158, 163, Robert Stenlake; p. 171, © Corbis; p. 172, © Christy's Images/Corbis

Publisher's Project Staff

Director, Product Development: Karen Dahlen; Associate Director, Product Development: Teri Mathews; Senior Editor: Patrick Keithahn; Editor: Jody Peterson; Development Assistant: Bev Johnson; Designer and Cover Illustrator: Denise Bunkert; Design Manager: Nancy Condon; Desktop Publishing Specialists: Pegi Cull, Linda Peterson; Desktop Publishing Manager: Lisa Beller; Purchasing Agent: Mary Kaye Kuzma; Executive Director of Marketing: Matt Keller; Marketing Manager: Brian Holl

Printed in the United States of America

ISBN 0-7854-2643-4

Product Number 91730

A 0 9 8 7 6 5 4 3 2 1

CONTENTS

◆ **Word Study Tips** 6

◆ **Chapter 1** 9

Lesson 1 "Flip-Flop: A Fine Dog," Part 1 10

Lesson 2 "Flip-Flop: A Fine Dog," Part 2 17

Lesson 3 "Into the Eye" 24

Lesson 4 "John Muir: The Father of Our National Parks" 31

Lesson 5 "Dear Journal" 38

Lesson 6 "Devil Down Under" 45

Lesson 7 "Making a Difference: Airline Ambassadors" 52

   Summary of Skills and Strategies 59

   Chapter 1 Review 60

◆ **Chapter 2** 67

Lesson 1 "Double Trouble," Part 1 68

Lesson 2 "Double Trouble," Part 2 75

Lesson 3 "Book Talk" 82

Lesson 4 "Out of This World Research," Part 1 89

Lesson 5 "Out of This World Research," Part 2 96

Lesson 6 "Slam Dunk" 103

Lesson 7 "As Far As the Eye Can See" 110

   Summary of Skills and Strategies 117

   Chapter 2 Review 118

◆ **Chapter 3** 125

Lesson 1 "*Learning Curve*," Part 1 126

Lesson 2 "*Learning Curve*," Part 2 133

Lesson 3 "*We're Not Alone*" 140

Lesson 4 "*Cicada Cycle*" 147

Lesson 5 "*A Talent to Lead*" 154

Lesson 6 "*A Man Ahead of His Time*" 161

Lesson 7 "*Teddy's Bear*" 168

Summary of Skills and Strategies 175

Chapter 3 Review 176

◆ **Word Bank** 183

◆ Welcome!

Reading is like anything else that matters. In order to be good at it, you have to practice.

Here is how *Reading Skills for Life* will help you become a better reader:

▶ **You will learn the sounds that letters stand for.** Knowing the sounds letters stand for lets you figure out new words by sounding them out.

▶ **You will get to know important words by sight.** Some words can't be sounded out. You just have to remember the way they look. Knowing lots of words by sight is one big key to reading.

▶ **You will know how words can change.** This book will help you see how words change, and what the changes mean.

▶ **You will read better by reading more.** You will read stories about characters who face real-life problems and find solutions. You will also learn some facts about the real world. (Some of these may surprise you!) And you will read about some real people who have done amazing things.

▶ **You will learn about yourself.** Your ideas are important! This book will help you think about what you read. What **you** think about what you read matters. This book gives you plenty of chances to "be the judge."

With a little practice, you'll be reading like a pro in no time! So start reading!

◆ The Five Steps to Learning a Word

1. **Read the word.** Notice its shape. Is it long or short? What letters does it begin with? Does it look like other words you know?

2. **Say the word.** What sounds does it have? Which letters stand for those sounds?

3. **Write the word.** Get a feel for the word by writing it down.

4. **Add the word to your Word Bank.** You will find a Word Bank in the back of this book. It has space for you to write the new words you learn. Your Word Bank lets you keep track of all the words you are learning.

5. **Practice reading the word.** Read the word again and again until you know it.

◀▶ Tips for Reading Longer Words

Short words are usually simple to read. It's easy to get stumped when you come to longer words. Here are some tips that can help:

▶ **Look for word parts you know.** Is the word made up of a smaller word you know, plus an ending?

▶ **Look for letter patterns you know.** If you know one pattern of letters, like the **ain** in **main,** use it when you come to other words. Knowing **main** can help you read lots of words you may not know, such as **pain, train, stained,** and **raining.**

▶ **Break the word into parts.** Is the word made up of two smaller words that have been put together?

▶ **Look for syllables.** The vowels in a word are a clue to how many syllables it has.

▶ **Think about the sounds the letters stand for.** Look at the letters in the word. What sounds do the letters stand for? Blend all the sounds together to read the word.

◀▶ Using Context Clues

Sometimes the other words in a sentence give you clues to a word's meaning. Here's an example:

> The **trunk** is locked, and Jim has the car keys.

What does **trunk** mean in this sentence?

    a. the back part of a car

    b. an elephant's nose

    c. a big box for clothes

The words **locked** and **car keys** are context clues. They help you see that here, **trunk** means "the back part of a car."

Look for context clues when you read. You can find them everywhere!

REMEMBER...
If you try one tip for reading a word and it doesn't work, try something else. If all else fails, use a dictionary. Or ask a friend for help.

CHAPTER 1

▶ **Lesson 1** . . . . *page 10*
   "Flip-Flop: A Fine Dog," Part 1

▶ **Lesson 2** . . . . *page 17*
   "Flip-Flop: A Fine Dog," Part 2

▶ **Lesson 3** . . . . *page 24*
   "Into the Eye"

▶ **Lesson 4** . . . . *page 31*
   "John Muir: The Father
   of Our National Parks"

▶ **Lesson 5** . . . . *page 38*
   "Dear Journal"

▶ **Lesson 6** . . . . *page 45*
   "Devil Down Under"

▶ **Lesson 7** . . . . *page 52*
   "Making a Difference:
   Airline Ambassadors"

Letters and Sounds

◆ **Directions:** These words have a short vowel sound. Circle the vowel or vowels in each word.

1. man   2. would   3. fin   4. kit   5. young

◆ **Directions:** These words have a long vowel sound. Circle the vowels in each word.

6. mane   7. fine   8. kite

▲ **TIPS:** ▶ If there are two vowels in a word and one is a final **e,** the first vowel usually stands for a long sound. The final **e** is silent.
▶ The words above have the consonant-vowel-consonant-**e** pattern. Another way to say consonant-vowel-consonant-**e** is CVC**e.**

◆ **Directions:** Write each word in the box where it belongs.

puppy	sought	crib	bread
tread	young	fed	gym
brought	shed	build	lick

short *u*	short *e*	short *i*	short *o*
9. _____	11. _____	15. _____	19. _____
10. _____	12. _____	16. _____	20. _____
	13. _____	17. _____	
	14. _____	18. _____	

▲ **TIPS:** ▶ The words **tread, young,** and **gym** have short vowel sounds. When vowels are combined, they may have the sound of one of the vowels, such as the short **e** sound in **tread** or the short **u** sound in **young.**
▶ The letter **y** can be any vowel sound, such as the short **i** sound in **gym** or the long **e** sound in **happy.**

◆ **Directions:** Write the letters on the lines. How many words can you make?

| p | br | s | tr |

21. _____ ead   23. _____ ick   27. _____ ought

22. _____ ead   24. _____ ick   28. _____ ought

25. _____ ick

26. _____ ick

Story Words

◆ **Directions:** Read each word to yourself. Then say the word out loud. Write the word on the line. Check the box after each step.

29. heard	Read ❑ Say ❑ Write ❑	_____
30. kennel (ken|nel)	Read ❑ Say ❑ Write ❑	_____
31. special (spe|cial)	Read ❑ Say ❑ Write ❑	_____
32. thought	Read ❑ Say ❑ Write ❑	_____
33. tongue	Read ❑ Say ❑ Write ❑	_____
34. shelter (shel|ter)	Read ❑ Say ❑ Write ❑	_____

More Word Work

You can add **ed** to many verbs. Do this to make a verb tell about the past.

Now: Kate **is calling** her dog.   The Past: Kate **called** her dog.

◆ **Directions:** Add **ed** to each word. Then write the word in the sentence.

Example: lick licked → Spot licked the boy.

35. brush _____ → Mark _____ his teeth.

36. look _____ → Bob _____ at the picture.

37. ask _____ → Mrs. Smith _____ a question.

◆ **Directions:** You know that you can add **s** or **es** to many words. Add **s** or **es** to each word below.

38. rush _____   **41.** size _____

39. door _____   **42.** box _____

40. dog _____   **43.** cage _____

▶ **TIP:** If a word ends with **x, ch, sh,** or **s,** add **es** instead of **s.**

Use What You Know

Luis gets his first dog. His Mom is not sure she will let him keep the dog. Have you ever had to persuade someone? Write about it on the lines below. Then read on to find out if Luis gets to keep his first dog.

_____

_____

_____

FLIP-FLOP: A FINE DOG, PART 1

Luis heard it first. There was barking and lots of it. During the drive, all he could think was, "Today is the big day. Today is the big day."

"Luis are you coming?" Mom asked as she pushed her purse strap up higher. "Part of me thinks this is crazy. You know I didn't have a dog as a kid."

"I know, I know," Luis said, smiling. "It's going to be great."

Walking around outside, **the barking hit Luis like a wave.** A man in a green canvas jumpsuit took them to the kennels. The furry faces stared out from the metal cages. "Wow, there are so many," Luis said.

"Take your time. They are all different, just like people. Each dog needs a good home. Choose with care," he said. "Some dogs need more space than others because they have to run around. Some dogs need to be trained or need special care."

There were dogs of every size. One was thin, with ears that stuck up. He hid in the back of his kennel. There were two tan-colored puppies

chewing on each other's tails. A huge dog growled at them, his lips appeared to curl back as he bared his teeth. Luis decided to keep looking.

"I like this one," Mom said. "He is so cute. I think it's a cocker spaniel. Mrs. Tillney, the woman next door, had one just like this."

"I don't know," said Luis. "He is too small."

Luis saw one with black, curly fur. Luis held his hand out. The puppy sat, her tail wagging on the bottom of the cage. Then she licked his hand. "Mom, she licked me! Mom, come see."

"She's nice, but she's a puppy," said the man. "Puppies need a lot of training. Her hair is long, too; she needs to be brushed often."

"I'll take good care of her," said Luis.

The man brought her out of the cage. Her whole body moved as she wagged her tail. She gave Luis another lick.

"Her name will be Flip-Flop," said Luis.

"How come?" asked Mom.

Luis knelt down and hugged his new dog. "Because her hair flip-flops over her eyes. Maybe she needs a trim."

Back at home, the first thing Mom did was take a picture. "Pop-whiz" went the instant camera and Luis held the picture by the corner. Soon a black, furry face and Luis's smile were looking back at him.

That night, Luis woke up twice just to see if it was really true. He had wanted a dog for such a long time. Once, Flip-Flop's legs moved while she slept. "Dogs dream too," thought Luis.

The next morning, Luis said, "Behave while I'm gone." Luis left Flip-Flop in the kitchen with some chew toys and a bone.

After school, Luis rushed home. His backpack landed with a thud as he stood by the back door. Something was wrong. "That looks like a hole in the door," Luis thought. Just then, he saw a red tongue and black fur sticking out. Flip-Flop barked and chewed some more.

"Flip-Flop, stop! Stop!" he called. He unlocked the door and Flip-Flop stood there shaking with delight. "What did you do to the kitchen? It's a mess!" It looked like a dozen monkeys had been there. Cereal boxes, pasta, and flour were spread out all over the floor. "Mom isn't going to like this!"

Luis tried to clean up, but Flip-Flop kept jumping on him. "Okay girl," he said, "I'll tie you to the tree, outside. I have to clean up. **Mom will flip.**"

Luis swept and wiped and tried to make the kitchen look normal. There was no way to fix the hole before Mom came home. He pushed out the back door and there, lying on the ground in the shape of a snake, was the leash, well, part of the leash. Flip-Flop was gone. "Where did she go?" asked Luis, spinning his head around. "Flip-Flop! FLIP-FLOP!" he called.

Luis looked up and down the hill his house was on. "Flip-Flop!" he called until his throat hurt, but she was nowhere.

Do you think Luis will find Flip-Flop? Circle your answer.

YES   NO

Then keep reading to find out what takes place.

Luis smelled dinner cooking. He could see light through the chewed hole. Mom turned around as he walked in, "Luis, we need to talk about Flip-Flop." Then her face dropped. "Where is she?"

Luis rubbed the leash between his fingers. "I had her tied up, Mom. Flip-Flop was right there. I had to clean up. Then I went outside to get her, and she wasn't there." Luis stared at the floor and bit his lip.

"Looks like she chewed it, just like she chewed the door," Mom said and crossed her arms. "I don't know if Flip-Flop is for us."

"I know she didn't behave today, but she will. I just have to find her. This is a problem I have to solve," Luis said, and then he thought of something. He pulled the picture from the night before off the refrigerator. "I'll show this to everyone who lives around here and ask them if they've seen her."

"That's too many people to speak to. Why don't you ask Riley to help you?" Luis's mother asked.

"Mom, Riley has to use a cane to walk."

"Not to walk with you, but to make posters."

Riley lived next door. Luis took the picture and walked next door. When he came out, he had a stack of posters. "Lost Dog. Please call Luis Soto at 555-1111. Reward."

Luis was awake before the sun came up. He shoved the stack of posters into his backpack and set off. He put posters on telephone poles, storefronts, and bulletin boards. After school, he called the shelter to see if Flip-Flop had run back there. "Sorry, but we'll **keep an eye out** for her," said the man.

Two days later, the phone rang. Luis picked up the phone.

"Hello, I'm trying to reach Luis Soto," said a woman.

"That's me." Luis gripped the phone.

"I think I may have your dog."

That night Mom said, "Luis, I don't think we can keep Flip-Flop. There are other dogs at the shelter. It's not easy to take care of puppies."

Flip-Flop wagged her tail until she shook. Luis brushed her black fur. "Mom, I want to keep Flip-Flop. I called the man at the animal shelter. I told him what Flip-Flop did. He said he will help me train her. I will have to help him with the dogs at the shelter. He is also bringing us a kennel for Flip-Flop."

"A kennel?" Mom asked. "A kennel is a metal cage to keep her in. So that when we are not here she can't make a mess of the house," Luis explained.

Mom hugged Flip-Flop, pushing her hair back. "We'll give you another chance, but no more doors for dinner," she warned. ▶

You Be the Judge

◆ 1. Do you think that Luis will be able to train Flip-Flop? Why or why not? Write what you think on the lines below.

_____

_____

2. If you were Luis, what would you say to persuade his mother to keep Flip-Flop? Explain.

_____

_____

Think About the Story

Use Story Words

◆ **Directions:** Look at your list of story words on page 11. Write a story word on each line.

3. When Luis _____ what his mother said about taking care of puppies, he _____ about what he would do to take care of Flip-Flop.

4. When Flip-Flop licked Luis, he felt a wet _____.

5. Pets without homes stay at the animal _____.

6. The man at the shelter said that some dogs may need _____ care.

7. When Flip-Flop is left alone, she will be spending time in a _____.

Write Sentences About the Story

◆ **Directions:** Circle the word that best fits in each sentence. Then write the sentence on the line.

8. Luis and Mom (goes/go) to the dog kennels.

_____

_____

9. Luis (names/name) his dog Flip-Flop.

_____

_____

When Did It Happen?

◆ 10. Write a number from 1 to 4 in front of each event to show the order in which it happened.

_____ Flip-Flop runs away.

_____ Luis chooses a dog carefully.

_____ A woman calls Luis to tell him she has found Flip-Flop.

_____ Flip-Flop chews a hole in the door.

Words and Meanings

◆ **Directions:** Think about how the **bold** words are used in the story. Then circle the words that show the meaning of each word or phrase.

11. Luis says, **"Mom will flip."** What does this mean?

    a. Mom will do a back flip.

    b. Mom will be upset about the mess.

    c. Mom will give the dog a haircut.

12. The man says, "We'll **keep an eye out** for her." This means that he _____.

    a. will help Luis hang posters to find Flip-Flop

    b. will keep one eye open

    c. will be looking for Flip-Flop at the shelter

13. **The barking hit Luis like a wave.** This means that _____.

    a. the barking was quiet

    b. the barking was very loud

    c. there was little barking

The Big Idea

14. Circle the sentence that sums up the story.

    a. Luis decides to help out at the animal shelter.

    b. Luis gets his first dog and has to convince his mother to let him keep her.

    c. Flip-Flop is a dog with black, curly hair.

Look Ahead

◆ 15. How do you think Flip-Flop will behave? What kinds of challenges will Luis face training Flip-Flop? Write what you think on the lines below. Read on to find out what happens.

_____

_____

Letters and Sounds

◆ **Directions:** These words have the long **e** sound. Circle the vowel or vowels in each word.

1. feet   2. peach   3. receive   4. shield   5. busy

> **TIP:** The letters **ee, ea, y, ey, e-e, ie,** and **ei** can all stand for the long **e** sound.

◆ **Directions:** Read these words. Circle each one that has the long **e** sound.

6. bee   9. achieve   12. handkerchief

7. silk   10. peacock   13. monkey

8. bell   11. cream   14. leaf

◆ **Directions:** Write each word you circled under the word below that has the same pattern of letters for long **e.**

need	flea	key	believe
15. _____	16. _____	19. _____	20. _____
	17. _____		21. _____
	18. _____		

◆ **Directions:** Write the letters on the lines. How many words can you make?

m	cr	d	bl	f	s

22. _____ eek   25. _____ eed   30. _____ eat

23. _____ eek   26. _____ eed   31. _____ eat

24. _____ eek   27. _____ eed   32. _____ eat

28. _____ eed   33. _____ eat

29. _____ eed

Story Words

◆ **Directions:** Read each word to yourself. Then say the word out loud. Write the word on the line. Check the box after each step.

34. whined   Read ❑ Say ❑ Write ❑ _____

35. whimpered   Read ❑ Say ❑ Write ❑ _____
   (whim | pered)

36. leash   Read ❑ Say ❑ Write ❑ _____

37. sneakers (sneak | ers)   Read ❑ Say ❑ Write ❑ _____

38. pamphlet   Read ❑ Say ❑ Write ❑ _____
   (pam | phlet)

39. session (ses | sion)   Read ❑ Say ❑ Write ❑ _____

Word Bank

Write each of these story words in the Word Bank at the back of this book.

More Word Work

You can make a noun mean more than one. This is called plural. To do this, add **s** or **es** to the ending.

Singular: Tom ate a cookie for dessert.
     The ball fell in the bush.

Plural: Tom ate two cookies for dessert.
    The ball fell in the bushes.

◆ **Directions:** Make each word plural. Then write the word in the sentence.

40. tent _____ → Four _____ are needed
         for the camping trip.

41. daisy _____ → The vase is full of _____.

42. box _____ → _____ were stacked in the
        moving van.

43. hoof _____ → Horses have _____.

> **TIP:** Add **es** to nouns ending in **sh, z, x,** or **ch** (sounding like **ch**). Change the **f** to a **v** before adding **s** or **es** in some nouns ending with **f.** Change the **y** to **i** and then add **es** to nouns ending in **y.**

Use What You Know

Luis is having difficulty getting Flip-Flop to sleep. How do you think you would feel if you weren't getting enough sleep?

_____

_____

_____

_____

FLIP-FLOP: A FINE DOG, PART 2

Luis pulled the pillow over his head. "Why won't you just go to sleep," he thought. "Flip-Flop, lie down and go to sleep!" Flip-Flop whined and whimpered, then nudged her head under Luis's pillow and tried to lick his face. "Flip-Flop, please," Luis complained. "I have a big test in the morning." Flip-Flop licked him again. "Okay, okay."

The time on the clock said 3:23 A.M. "All right, girl, if you really need to go outside, but then it will be time to sleep." Luis rolled out of bed and stumbled to turn the light on. Flip-Flop shook so hard she fell over, and then she jumped back up, ready to go.

Outside, Luis held the leash and walked her around the backyard. Flip-Flop sniffed by the tree and along the edge of the fence. She pulled at the leash and grunted with each new smell. He heard the back door open and saw his mother leaning out the door.

"Luis, it's the middle of the night. Did you wake up Flip-Flop again?"

"No, Mom," Luis said, "She woke me up again."

"You know, son," Mom said. "When you were a baby, I was up every night for six months. I was so tired. One day I went to work with two different shoes on."

"It's a good thing I only wear sneakers," Luis replied.

The next day at school, Luis felt **like his brain had turned to molasses.** He yawned and rubbed his cheeks as he sat in class. "It's so warm in here," he thought. "I just have to make it through this test."

His friend, Brad, leaned over and whispered, "Luis, wake up, man. Mr. Delaney is passing out the tests. After school we're meeting at the park for a **pick-up game of hoops.** Maybe you can come?"

"Maybe," Luis replied, "after a nap."

After school, Flip-Flop wiggled and wagged her tail when Luis got home. "Ruff, ruff," she barked.

"Flip-Flop, thanks to you, my test didn't go well today." Flip-Flop wagged her tail even harder, and everything shook inside the kennel.

After a short walk around the yard, Luis brought Flip-Flop back in the house. He lay down on the couch and soon fell asleep. He didn't hear the chewing in the corner.

"Luis, I'm home," Mom called. "Oh no, Flip-Flop."

Hanging from Flip-Flop's mouth was a sneaker—that is, what was left of a sneaker. The lace was completely gone and the rubber sole was full of teeth marks.

"You ate the whole lace," groaned Mom, pulling the shoes out of Flip-Flop's mouth.

"My sneakers. How are we going to get you to stop chewing and to sleep through the night?" Luis asked Flip-Flop, scratching her under her chin. "Mom, guess what else Flip-Flop likes to eat?"

"I don't think I want to know."

"Ice. She loves ice. She chews each piece and rolls it around in her mouth. That's the only trick she can do so far, though."

"That reminds me," Mom said. She pulled a pamphlet out of her purse and handed it to Luis. "Flip-Flop has to learn how to behave."

The pamphlet was called "The Dog Zone: **When You Don't Have a Century to Teach Fido to Fetch.**"

"I called your friend at the animal shelter. He told me about this school," Mom explained. "You'll have to take her once a week for the whole session."

"Thanks, Mom." Luis said. "Now it's your turn to go to school, Flip-Flop."

 Do you think Flip-Flop will learn how to behave? Circle your answer.

YES   NO

Keep reading to find out what takes place.

The following Tuesday afternoon, Luis walked into town. The sun was shining and leaves spun down and around. Flip-Flop chased as many leaves as she could, yanking Luis back and forth. They passed the Village Veggie Mart and came to a glass door with a sign painted on it in bright orange letters, "The Dog Zone."

Inside, about a half dozen people waited with their dogs. The dog owners all looked nervous as they held onto leashes and tried to keep their dogs from getting too close to one another. Flip-Flop wagged her tail and pulled hard. "Stop, Flip-Flop." Luis tugged back, feeling the heat rise on his neck. "Can they kick a dog out of training class?" he wondered.

"Welcome to The Dog Zone. My name is Buck," said a man. "Be firm, but do not rush. These are the first things you need to think of when training a dog." Buck brought a dog out of a kennel and walked her around on a leash. "Heel," he said, and the dog walked close by him as they circled the room. "Sit," he said, and the dog looked at him.

"Sit," he said in a deeper voice, and the dog sat. Afterwards, he gave the dog a nice pat and fed her a small dog bone.

"You can buy treats and give them to your dogs if they do a good job. Always give your dogs praise by petting them and telling them they are good when they do something you have asked," Buck explained. "Today we will start with training the dog to walk on a leash."

An older woman with a large red dog tried to get it to move. The dog looked like it was stuck to the floor. It just sat there. It refused to walk. Another dog pulled so hard she made her owner trip. Flip-Flop walked, tugging on the leash and trying to say hello to the other dogs. "Keep moving girl," Luis said under his breath.

"If your dog is doing what you want, ease up on the leash. If it's tight all the time, your dog won't know right from wrong. Remember to use the same words or commands," Buck said.

Each week Buck taught Luis more about how to handle Flip-Flop. Each week she behaved better, but she still wasn't letting Luis sleep.

After class one day, Luis went over to Buck. Buck knelt down and gave Flip-Flop a scratch behind her ears. She shook with happiness. "You've got a real nice dog here, Luis," said Buck.

"Thanks, but she won't sleep through the night," Luis explained.

"Activity," Buck said flatly. "Flip-Flop needs exercise and lots of it. She is a growing puppy and needs to run. Run around the park. Run, run, run."

That night Luis took the long way home. In the beginning Flip-Flop ran a step ahead of Luis. At the end she was panting and was working to keep up. That night both Flip-Flop and Luis slept through the whole night.

You Be the Judge

◆ 1. Why do you think Luis's mom thinks Flip-Flop should go to school? Write what you think on the lines below.

_____

_____

2. Do you think the training session at The Dog Zone was helpful to Luis and Flip-Flop? Explain.

_____

_____

Think About the Story

Use Story Words

◆ **Directions:** Look at your list of story words on page 18. Write a story word on each line.

3. Flip-Flop _____ to go out at night.

4. Flip-Flop also _____ at Luis and nudged his pillow.

5. Mom signed up Luis and Flip-Flop for a _____ of dog training.

6. If Flip-Flop behaves on her _____ Luis should praise her.

7. Flip-Flop chewed Luis's _____ .

8. Mom pulled a _____ from her purse.

How Did They Feel?

◆ **Directions:** Read the sentence from the story. Write a sentence to describe how Luis was feeling at that time.

9. "Stop, Flip-Flop," Luis tugged back, feeling the heat rise on his neck. "Can they kick a dog out of training class?" he wondered.

_____

_____

10. That night both Flip-Flop and Luis slept through the whole night.

_____

_____

Words and Meanings

Directions: Think about how the **bold** words are used in the story. Then circle the answer that shows the meaning of each word or phrase.

11. Luis felt **like his brain had turned to molasses.** What does this mean?

    a. Luis was thinking slowly.

    b. Luis was falling asleep at his desk.

    c. Luis couldn't speak.

12. Brad said, "We're meeting at the park for a **pick-up game of hoops.**" This means _____.

    a. there is basketball practice after school

    b. a number of kids are going to play a game of basketball after school

    c. Brad and his friends are playing with hula-hoops at the park

13. The Dog Zone pamphlet described the dog school as a place to go **"When You Don't Have a Century to Teach Fido to Fetch."** This means _____.

    a. your dog will be trained quickly at The Dog Zone

    b. it takes one hundred years to train a dog

    c. dogs cannot be trained

Write Sentences About the Story

Directions: Use words from the story to answer these questions.

14. Why is Luis tired at school?

    _____

    _____

15. What does Luis do to get Flip-Flop to sleep through the night?

    _____

    _____

The Big Idea

16. Circle the sentence that sums up the story.

    a. Luis is disappointed by his performance on the test.

    b. Luis's mom stayed up with him when he was a baby.

    c. Luis takes Flip-Flop to dog training school and she learns how to behave better.

Letters and Sounds

◆ **Directions:** These words have the long **a** sound. Circle the letters that make the long **a** sound in each word.

1. tray   2. face   3. daisy   4. aim

> **TIP:** The letters **a, ai, ay, ei, ea, eigh,** and **ey** can all make the long **a** sound. The long **a** sound is spelled **ai** in **daisy**.

◆ **Directions:** Read these words. Circle each one that has the long **a** sound.

5. great   8. fell   11. spike

6. snake   9. away   12. grape

7. peal   10. lady   13. sleigh

◆ **Directions:** Write each word you circled under the word below that has the same pattern for long **a.**

weigh	scrape	tray	steak
14. _____	15. _____ 16. _____ 17. _____	18. _____	19. _____

◆ **Directions:** Write the letters on the lines. How many words can you make?

s	pr	c	sl	w	tr	p	t	b

20. _____ ay   26. _____ eigh   28. _____ ake

21. _____ ay   27. _____ eigh   29. _____ ake

22. _____ ay   30. _____ ake

23. _____ ay   31. _____ ake

24. _____ ay   32. _____ ake

25. _____ ay

Story Words

Directions: Read each word to yourself. Then say the word out loud. Write the word on the line. Check the box after each step.

33. virtual (vir | tu | al) Read ❑ Say ❑ Write ❑ _____

34. typhoon (ty | phoon) Read ❑ Say ❑ Write ❑ _____

35. predict (pre | dict) Read ❑ Say ❑ Write ❑ _____

36. debate (de | bate) Read ❑ Say ❑ Write ❑ _____

37. intensify Read ❑ Say ❑ Write ❑ _____
  (in | ten | si | fy)

38. data (da | ta) Read ❑ Say ❑ Write ❑ _____

More Word Work

You can change the meaning of a word by changing its ending. Add **er** to make a word mean **more**. Add **est** to make a word mean **the most**. Raquel has a **clean** locker.
Raquel's locker is **cleaner** than Stephan's locker.
Raquel's locker is the **cleanest** of all the lockers.

Directions: Make each word mean "more." Add **er**. Then write the word in the sentence.

Example: big bigger → A grapefruit is bigger than an egg.

39. high _____ → The American flag flies
_____ than the state flag.

40. loose _____ → Untie your shoe to make it
_____.

Directions: Make each word mean "the most." Add **est.** Then write the word in the sentence.

Example: wise wisest → Benjamin Franklin was one of the
wisest men in the eighteenth century.

41. tall _____ → Redwoods are some of the
_____ trees.

42. fast _____ → Cheetahs are the _____
runners in the animal kingdom.

TIP: Use an adjective that ends in **er,** also called a **comparative** adjective, when you compare two things. When you compare more than two things, use an adjective that ends in **est,** which is called a **superlative.**

Use What You Know

In this selection, you will learn about hurricanes and how scientists research this kind of weather. What do you already know about this type of storm? Write about it on the lines below.

_____

_____

_____

_____

INTO THE EYE

A seat belt cuts against your legs. High-speed winds whip by. You wish you hadn't eaten that second slice of pizza. The white stuff surrounding you looks almost like snow, but you know it isn't. There is no turning back, no changing your mind. You have committed to the trip. Are you riding a tall and fast roller coaster? No. Have you strapped on a virtual helmet and paid for a computer-driven thrill? No. You are in for the fastest ride of your life on a turboprop plane **charting a course** directly through the eye of a hurricane.

Hurricanes are storms with extremely strong, swirling winds. They form over water when many thunderstorms join together to make clusters. Low pressure in the middle causes air to rise. More air rushes in. The faster the wind flows through this cycle, the worse the storm. For a storm to even count as a hurricane, it has to have winds that blow at least 74 miles per hour (119 km/h). In the most powerful hurricanes, winds can reach 180 miles per hour (300 km/h).

The name "hurricane" comes from the West Indian word "huracan," which means "big wind." Hurricanes form over the Atlantic and eastern Pacific Oceans. These storms have different names in other parts of the world. Western Pacific storms are called typhoons, from the Chinese word "taifun," which means "great wind." In Australia, a hurricane is called "willy-willy."

Hurricanes are circular in shape, and they can be hundreds of miles across. Mighty winds and wide strips of clouds swirl or spiral toward the center. At the very center is the "eye," where there is calm, and often blue sky. This is surprising, considering the power of the rest of the storm.

Scientists already know a great deal about the patterns of these storms. They move with wind currents of an average speed of 16 mph (26 km/h). Some hurricanes move at twice this speed and some stay in the same spot for many days.

Predicting exactly where hurricanes will go and how strong they will be is a challenge. Hurricanes create strong waves at sea and tides that damage the coast. Homes, businesses, trees, and people suffer. In 1992, Hurricane Andrew surprised many people when it quickly hit the shores of Southern Florida, killing 15 people. The more they know about what causes hurricanes and their movements, the better they will be at warning people of them.

In the North Atlantic these tropical storms occur most often during the late summer and early fall. This is because of high humidity and warm waters. Humidity is the amount of water in the air. This area of the world usually experiences about five storms big enough to be called hurricanes each year.

At MacDill Air Force Base in Tampa, Florida, there is a plane called "Miss Piggy." **On her side Miss Piggy sports dozens of red hurricane-shaped stickers,** each with a name of a storm she has flown through. She is a turboprop plane. She is used instead of a jet because she gets more lift in the tricky winds of a hurricane.

Why would anyone want to travel to the center of one of these storms? Scientists and weather experts do it to gather information.

Scientists continue to debate what causes a hurricane to intensify or get worse, and why it will follow a certain path.

Do you think you would like to be on a hurricane research plane? Circle your answer.

YES   NO

Then keep reading to find out how they learn more about hurricanes.

Major factors that control a hurricane are how warm or cold the winds and the oceans are. Scientists develop hurricane models by looking at how warm or cold the wind and ocean are. As more is known, chances improve for warning people living along the coast.

On board Miss Piggy, there are many computers and four different radars that collect information, or data. There is more equipment that is shot out of the belly of the plane. At the beginning of a mission, the research team charts a course across the hurricane, through the eye, across the other side, up, and then back across. The map looks like a star. There are points on the star where they plan to drop their equipment.

One kind of equipment they drop is called a "Global Positioning Systems drop wind-sonde." There is a tube in the floor of the plane where the wind-sonde is placed. The air pressure inside the plane when it is flying is so much higher than it is outside that it pushes the wind-sonde out. Once the wind-sonde is a distance away from the plane, a parachute opens and the winds of the hurricane push it around. The Global Positioning System, or "GPS," sends signals back to the plane. These signals give its exact position at each moment. After many wind-sondes are dropped, researchers can see where the hurricane takes them. Then they are able to make a map of the hurricane.

The other type of equipment that is dropped is called an "Airborne Expendable Bathythermograph," or "AXBT." AXBTs fall all the way down to the ocean. When they hit water they release a thermometer. The thermometer is on a wire. Each AXBT's job after falling to 900 ft (275 m) is to find out how warm or cold the ocean is. Then they send these readings to the plane.

When Miss Piggy flew through Hurricane Dennis, 30 GPS wind-sondes were dropped and 15 AXBTs were launched. While all this work was done from the inside of the hurricane, other experts were also tracking wave data.

Flights like these may be exciting, but you, too, should be warned. They usually last longer than a school day. If you ever have the chance to take a ride through a hurricane's eye, you might want to think carefully before you say yes.

You Be the Judge

◆ 1. How do you think information collected from the inside of the storm is different from that gathered outside? Write what you think on the lines below.

_____

_____

Think About the Story

Use Story Words

◆ **Directions:** Look at your list of story words on page 25. Write a story word on each line.

2. Computers have made it possible to play _____ games.

3. Scientists use _____ to learn more about hurricanes.

4. Another word for hurricane is _____.

5. Weather experts try to _____ the weather.

6. The warmer the ocean water, the more a hurricane will _____.

7. Scientists and experts _____ or discuss the cause of hurricanes.

What Are the Facts?

◆ **Directions:** Write **T** next to the sentences that say true things about hurricanes. Write **F** next to the sentences that do not.

8. _____ Hurricanes are stronger over cold water.

9. _____ Windspeed affects hurricanes.

10. _____ Hurricane research is done in jet planes.

11. _____ Another word for hurricane is willy-willy.

12. _____ Hurricanes can sit in one place for days.

What Can You Tell?

13. How does the temperature of ocean water affect a hurricane? Write what you think on the lines below.

_____

_____

Words and Meanings

Directions: Think about how the **bold** words are used in the story. Then circle the words that show the meaning of each word or phrase.

14. The plane was **charting a course** directly through the eye of the hurricane. What does this phrase mean?
    a. The plane was flying toward the eye.
    b. The plane was avoiding the hurricane.
    c. The plane was trying to circle the storm.

15. If a research plane **sports stickers on her side,** this means _____.
    a. something has been painted over
    b. the plane is used to fly professional hockey teams to games
    c. something is proudly and openly displayed on the side of the plane

Write Sentences About the Story

Directions: Use words from the story to answer these questions.

16. What is a hurricane?

_____

_____

17. Where does a hurricane form? What shape is it? What is at its center?

_____

_____

_____

18. What kind of information is gathered by the equipment dropped by Miss Piggy?

_____

_____

_____

Letters and Sounds

◆ **Directions:** These words have the long **i** sound. Circle the letter or letters that stand for the long **i** in each word.

1. fright   2. pie   3. spy   4. pirate

> **TIP:** The letters **y, i, ie, igh,** and **i-e** can all stand for the long **i** sound. Some words like **bridle** and **title** have the long **i** sound in the vowel-consonant-consonant-vowel, V/CCV pattern.

◆ **Directions:** Read these words. Circle each one that has the long **i** sound.

5. fly	8. gel	11. child
6. light	9. whistle	12. scrap
7. rice	10. night	13. mice

◆ **Directions:** Write each word you circled under the word below that has the same pattern of letters for long **i.**

try	knight	nine	silent
14. _____	15. _____	17. _____	19. _____
	16. _____	18. _____	

◆ **Directions:** Write the letters on the lines. How many words can you make?

m	fr	p	s	t	sp	n

20. _____ ight   25. _____ y

21. _____ ight   26. _____ y

22. _____ ight   27. _____ y

23. _____ ight

24. _____ ight

28. _____ ite

29. _____ ite

30. _____ ite

Story Words

◆ **Directions:** Read each word to yourself. Then say the word out loud. Write the word on the line. Check the box after each step.

31. explore (ex | plore) Read ❑ Say ❑ Write ❑ _____

32. nature (na | ture) Read ❑ Say ❑ Write ❑ _____

33. conserve (con | serve) Read ❑ Say ❑ Write ❑ _____

34. preserve (pre | serve) Read ❑ Say ❑ Write ❑ _____

35. ideas (i | de | as) Read ❑ Say ❑ Write ❑ _____

36. reservoir Read ❑ Say ❑ Write ❑ _____
    (res | er | voir)

Word Bank

Write each of these story words in the Word Bank at the back of this book.

More Word Work

> **TIP:** You can usually make a word mean more than one, or plural, by adding an **s** to the end of it. However, this is not true for some words. These are called irregular plurals. To make these words mean more than one, you have to follow special rules.
>
> | Examples: | singular | plural |
> |---|---|---|
> | | spy | spies |
> | | life | lives |
> | | potato | potatoes |
> | | goose | geese |

◆ **Directions:** Make each word plural. Then write the word in the sentence.

Example: story stories → Newspapers are filled with stories.

37. cry _____ → The _____ of the

    twins woke him.

38. hero _____ → People who help others are

    _____.

39. half _____ → Use a knife to cut oranges into

    _____.

40. calf _____ → Runners develop strong

    _____.

Use What You Know

In this selection, you will read about John Muir. He had many great ideas that put him ahead of his time. He is best known for his work to protect the environment. What are some ways people can help our environment today? Write your ideas on the lines below.

_____

_____

_____

_____

JOHN MUIR: THE FATHER OF OUR NATIONAL PARKS

As you read this, somewhere in our nation someone is walking through the woods. Someone is climbing a rock face, or sleeping snugly in a sleeping bag, enjoying the smell of evergreen trees. That person probably has John Muir to thank for the chance to explore and enjoy nature.

Muir did many things. He was at different times a farmer and a sheepherder. He was also an inventor, an explorer, and a writer. But most of all, he cared deeply for the natural world. Muir wrote that "the clearest way into the Universe is through a forest wilderness." But Muir saw how people treated the world for their own selfish reasons. Muir was ahead of his time because he learned to realize how important it was to care for our environment.

Muir was born on April 21, 1838 in Dunbar, a Scottish town on the stormy coast of the North Sea. He lived there until he was 11. Then, in 1849, the Muir family moved to the United States. They settled in Wisconsin and became farmers.

Muir's father was a strict parent with his children. When John was not in bed or at school, he was supposed to do farm work. Whenever he and his brother found any free time, they explored the countryside. They liked walking the fields and looking at wildflowers. They ran through the woods and climbed trees. They would squat by the creeks and try to catch crayfish.

When he was 22, Muir began classes at the University of Wisconsin. He was a good student, but after three years, his desire to see the world pushed him to travel. Slowly but surely, Muir walked his way through the northern United States and Canada. When he ran out of money, he would stop to do odd jobs.

While working at a carriage parts shop in Indianapolis, Indiana, Muir suffered an injury and lost his sight in one eye for a month. The accident made Muir think about the world in a new way. It was during this time that Muir decided to devote his life to nature.

Muir spent years exploring. He walked a thousand miles to the Gulf of Mexico. He continued to explore, sailing on to the countries of Cuba and Panama. In the spring of 1868, he docked in San Francisco, California. Muir was **quite taken** with this area. He was quite struck by the beauty of the Sierra Nevada mountain range and the area of Yosemite. He described that area as "the Range of Light . . . the most . . . beautiful of all the mountain chains I have ever seen."

Muir loved the land. He wished to understand it and to conserve it. He visited Alaska many times to study and write about glaciers. He traveled on to Australia, South America, Africa, Europe, China, and Japan. Muir once wrote, "Keep close to Nature's heart . . . and break clear away, once in awhile, and climb a mountain or spend a week in the woods. **Wash your spirit clean.**"

Muir's love of nature and his hope of conserving it led him to publish 300 articles and 10 books. With every word he wrote, Muir made a case to preserve the nation's natural wonders.

> **How do you think John Muir was unusual for his time? Write what you think on the lines below. Then keep reading to learn more about how Muir helped nature in America.**
>
> _____
>
> _____
>
> _____
>
> _____

In the late 1880s, Muir wrote his ideas about nature in *Century* magazine. He described how sheep and cattle were harming the meadows and forests near Yosemite. In 1890 Congress decided to create Yosemite National Park in California. This was not the only park Muir helped make. He also worked to create the Sequoia, Mount Ranier, Petrified Forest, and Grand Canyon national parks.

President Theodore Roosevelt read a copy of Muir's book, *Our National Parks.* He was **so moved** by the book that he visited Muir at Yosemite in 1903. They spoke at length in the beautiful forest. Together they made plans to conserve land. This is how Muir became known as the "Father of Our National Park System."

In *Our National Parks,* Muir said, "Climb the mountains and get their good tidings. Nature's peace will flow into you as sunshine flows into trees. The winds will blow their own freshness into you, and the storms their energy, while **cares will drop off like autumn leaves.**"

Even as national parks were being created, some people still wanted to use the land for different reasons. Muir and others founded the Sierra Club in 1892 to protect Yosemite National Park. During this time he battled against the damming of the Hetch Hetchy Valley within Yosemite. Muir was one of the country's first leaders for the environment. After years of effort, Muir and the Sierra Club lost the battle. A dam was built to create a reservoir to hold water for San Francisco.

Muir died in 1914, but his ideas still affect our lifes. He was a man ahead of his time, working to conserve land for everyone all over the country. The Sierra Club is still active, and in the year 2000, supported restoring the ecosystem of the Everglades in Florida. The Sierra Club also runs programs in parks and schools to help children understand how important it is to conserve nature.

If you ever find yourself laughing as you paddle a white-water raft through a river in the Grand Canyon, or trying not to look down as you rock climb in Yosemite, don't forget to thank John Muir. He is truly one of the great heroes of American history.

You Be the Judge

◆ 1. Why do you think John Muir spent much of his life traveling? Write what you think on the lines below.

_____

_____

2. How do you think a national park system benefits our nation? Write what you think on the lines below.

_____

_____

Think About the Story

Use Story Words

◆ **Directions:** Look at your list of story words on page 32. Write a story word on each line.

3. A _____ is a man-made lake used to store water.

4. John Muir wanted to _____ and _____ land.

5. John Muir loved _____.

6. Through writing, Muir shared his _____.

7. Two things Muir liked to do were travel and _____.

Write Sentences About the Story

◆ **Directions:** Use words from the story to answer these questions.

8. What was John Muir's favorite place?

_____

_____

9. How did Muir let people know about the importance of conserving nature?

_____

10. What action did Congress take to protect Yosemite?

_____

11. What action did Muir and others take to further protect Yosemite?

_____

Words and Meanings

Directions: Think about how the **bold** words are used in the story. Then circle the words that show the meaning of each word or phrase.

12. Muir was **"quite taken"** with California. This phrase means _____.
    a. he disliked California
    b. he loved California
    c. he did not care

13. Muir felt that spending a week in the woods would **"Wash your spirit clean."** What does this sentence mean?
    a. You will be at peace with yourself and nature.
    b. You will feel confused.
    c. You will not need a bath when you get home.

14. President Roosevelt was **"so moved"** by Muir's book means _____.
    a. the President liked the book very much
    b. the President thought the book could use more work
    c. the President did not finish the book

15. In one of his books Muir wrote that climbing makes **"cares drop off like autumn leaves."** This means that _____.
    a. you will worry about school when you are in the mountains
    b. you will not worry about everyday things when climbing
    c. you will be afraid when climbing a mountain

The Big Idea

16. Circle the sentence that sums up the story.
    a. John Muir moved to America when he was eleven.
    b. John Muir was a man who loved exploring the mountains.
    c. John Muir was a man with great ideas who helped create our National Park System.

When Did It Happen?

17. Write a number from 1 to 4 in front of each event to show when it happened.

    _____ Muir walked a thousand miles to the Gulf of Mexico.

    _____ The Sierra Club was created.

    _____ Muir and his brother walked the fields of Wisconsin.

    _____ John Muir met with President Roosevelt.

Letters and Sounds

◆ **Directions:** These words have the long **o** sound. Circle the letters that stand for the long **o** sound in each word.

1. tow   2. boat   3. home   4. though

> **TIP:** The letters **o, oa, ough, oe,** and **ow** can all stand for the long **o** sound.

◆ **Directions:** Read these words. Circle each one that has the long **o** sound.

5. crow	9. arrow	13. float
6. thorough	10. flower	14. dot
7. roast	11. dough	15. tough
8. telephone	12. pine	16. low

◆ **Directions:** Write each word you circled under the word below that has the same pattern of letters for the long **o**.

blow	zone	although	boast
17. _____	20. _____	21. _____	23. _____
18. _____		22. _____	24. _____
19. _____			

◆ **Directions:** Write the letters on the lines to make words with the long **o** sound.

bl	gl	thr	l	tr	fl

25. _____ oat	29. _____ one	31. _____ ow
26. _____ oat	30. _____ one	32. _____ ow
27. _____ oat		33. _____ ow
28. _____ oat		34. _____ ow
		35. _____ ow

Story Words

◆ **Directions:** Read each word to yourself. Then say the word out loud. Write the word on the line. Check the box after each step.

36. journal (jour | nal)   Read ❑ Say ❑ Write ❑   _____

37. cafeteria   Read ❑ Say ❑ Write ❑   _____
      (caf | e | te | ria)

38. algebra (al | ge | bra) Read ❑ Say ❑ Write ❑   _____

39. personal   Read ❑ Say ❑ Write ❑   _____
      (per | son | al)

40. juggling (jug | gling) Read ❑ Say ❑ Write ❑   _____

41. seriously   Read ❑ Say ❑ Write ❑   _____
      (se | ri | ous | ly)

More Word Work

You can add **'s** to show that a thing belongs to someone or has a connection to someone. This is called the possessive form.

◆ **Directions:** Add **e's** to each word to make it possessive. For words that already end in **s,** just add **'**. Then write the word to complete the sentence.

Example: Tom Tom's → That is Tom's house.

42. Barby _____ → They are _____
      earrings.

43. boys _____ → The _____ toys are all
      over the floor.

44. sister _____ → Please feed my _____
      cat.

45. friends _____ → My _____ games are
      fun.

Use What You Know

This story is about a girl named Julie who is in a new school. She would like to make some friends and writes about it in her journal. A journal is a place to write anything you want. What would you write in a journal about your life? Write what you think on the lines below.

_____

_____

_____

_____

DEAR JOURNAL

Dear Journal,

I'll have to sit by myself again. I've been at this school for two weeks and every day something worse happens in this cafeteria. I'll try for a table in the middle. I found out the second day that the window tables are all taken. The basketball players sit at the rectangle table by the glowing EXIT sign. The chit-chat group, a bunch of girls who can't stop talking, sit at the round table by the last window. They even asked me to move one day. "Excuse us," they said grinning and poking at one another, "this is our spot." I felt my face get **as hot as a baked potato.** That table is the best. It's so bright and warm in the sun. There is even a tree just on the other side of the glass. I decided it was better to move than make a scene.

Today everyone is shoving in this line. I have got to get through it so I can get a table. One day I sat on the floor and just wrote in my journal. I wonder what today's soup is? Eeew, that must be what smells so bad. It looks like it came out of a slimy lake.

"How about some split-pea soup?" a server asked while I was still writing. She stood there with a big yellow smock with a capital *R* sewn on it.

"No thanks," I said. "What does the *R* stand for?"

She paused and then smiled. "*R* is for Rose. Thanks for asking. How about a chicken patty? You've got to put some meat on those bones."

"Okay, I'll give it a try." I bet if I eat it with ketchup it might be okay. My method is to put the ketchup on the side. I like anything gloppy on the side.

I fish for the $2.65 in my purse. Then I rush for one of the open tables. Okay, I'll have room for my tray and room for my journal.

Dear Journal,

I'm so glad no one has asked me to move. Moving to a new school in the middle of the winter is the pits. Maybe I'll make a friend when the snow thaws. I think I have a chance at getting an A in algebra class. Mr. Slater is nice enough, but how can anyone be so into math? He got all excited this morning. "Now will you look at this," he almost yelled. "The curve will just keep going on and on until infinity." I wanted to say, "Whoa, slow down."

"Hey what are your writing? Hey I'm talking to you."

I look up. "Uh, me? Oh this is my journal. It's no big deal. Just some personal stuff." Bam, I close it up as fast as I can. Later on, someone walks over to me in the cafeteria.

"That's cool. My name's Kesia," she says stressing the *sh*. "We're in the same algebra class."

Now I remember her. One day she wore bright pink boots with heels. Today she has on a purple shirt with sequins sewn all over it. I don't think I'd wear a shirt like hers, but she is being friendly. I guess I shouldn't be picky. "Yes, algebra class. Has Mr. Slater been this excited about math all year?"

"Totally. One day he was talking about equations or something or other, I don't get math, and he actually," Kesia says leaning over the table, "hopped up on top of his desk trying to get us excited. I think he's a little crazy."

"I'd like to have seen that," I say.

"What a sight," she says, tapping her long nails on the table. Then she looks up and frowns. "Don't turn around now!"

Now when someone tells you with a surprised look on her face not to turn around, what do you do?

"Kesia check this out," a tall, muscular boy says. He holds an empty tray up on one finger, like a basketball. Then he uses his other hand to spin it around.

Kesia whispers, "That's Gerald. He's such a show-off. I think he's still mad I wouldn't go to the Harvest Moon Dance with him."

Will Gerald sit down with the two girls? Circle your answer.

YES   NO

Then read on to find out.

"Big deal, Gerald. We're busy here. Leave us be," Kesia spouts.

Gerald doesn't stop, he keeps spinning the tray. Somebody begins to clap.

Should I or shouldn't I, I ask myself. What have I got to lose? I grab three juice boxes and start. At first it's a little hard to do. I haven't done it in a while, but then the boxes are going faster. Up and over and back in my hand, I'm juggling. People start clapping for me.

"Hey that's pretty good. What's your name?" asks Gerald.

"Julie, I just moved here," I reply.

"Welcome. We could use a juggler. Oh, my fries are getting cool. Gotta go."

I sit back down and feel an excited warmth within me.

"Thanks for making him move on. I'm glad to see that you don't take yourself seriously," Kesia says smiling. "So how do you like math?"

"It's okay. I'm pretty good at it. I'm trying for an A. Math usually helps my averages. It's history that's hard for me. All those dates and names and wars. **I can't keep them at all straight.**"

"Do you think you could help me study for the math test on Thursday?" Kesia asks.

"Sure," I tell her.

That night I write in my journal.

Dear Journal,

I made a friend before the snow thawed. Kesia is really nice, as long as you can get used to the tapping of those long fingernails. I wonder how she types on a keyboard with them? Anyhow, we studied for the math test on Thursday. I feel like I learned as much as she did by teaching it to her. I don't have to worry about lunch tomorrow either. We are going to sit in the cafeteria together.

You Be the Judge

◆ 1. If you were Julie, what would you have done when Gerald was spinning the tray and your new friend wanted him to stop? Write what you think on the lines below.

_____

_____

2. Why do you think Julie writes in a journal? Explain.

_____

_____

Think About the Story

Use Story Words

◆ **Directions:** Look at your list of story words on page 39. Write a story word on each line.

3. Julie likes to write in her _____.

4. _____ with juice boxes can make a mess.

5. Rose works in the _____ as a server.

6. Kesia is having a hard time understanding _____.

7. When you take something _____, you feel it is important.

8. Julie writes about things that are _____.

Write Sentences About the Story

◆ **Directions:** Use words from the story to answer these questions.

9. Why does Julie feel bad every day in the cafeteria?

_____

_____

10. What does Julie want to make her feel less lonely?

_____

11. What does Julie do that impresses Kesia?

_____

12. Why doesn't Julie have to worry about lunch anymore?

_____

Words and Meanings

Directions: Think about how the **bold** words are used in the story. Then circle the words that show the meaning of each word or phrase.

13. Julie felt her face get **"as hot as a baked potato."** This means Julie was _____.

    a. happy

    b. scared

    c. embarrassed

14. Julie wrote "moving to a new school. . . **is the pits.**" What did she mean?

    a. Starting at a new school can be hard.

    b. She thinks she will like this school.

    c. Starting at a new school is not so bad.

15. Julie says, **"I can't keep them at all straight."** This means that _____.

    a. she gets confused

    b. she draws straight lines

    c. she knows all her facts

What Can You Tell?

16. Do you think Julie and Kesia will become good friends? Why or why not? Write about it on the lines below.

    _____

    _____

How Did They Feel?

17. How did Julie feel when she was waiting in line for her food? Explain.

    _____

    _____

18. How do you think Julie's mood changes during the story? Explain.

    _____

    _____

Letters and Sounds

◆ **Directions:** These words have the long **u** sound. Circle the long **u** sound in each word.

1. clue   2. food   3. blew   4. through

> **TIP:** The letters **u, ue, oo, ew, ou,** and **ough** can all stand for the long **u** sound. Words like **food** and **clue** have the vowel-vowel pattern. Another way to say vowel-vowel is V/V.

◆ **Directions:** Read these words. Circle each one that has the long **u** sound.

5. crew   8. lute   11. sap   14. true

6. block   9. goose   12. mushroom   15. parachute

7. loon   10. ripe   13. group   16. bull

◆ **Directions:** Use the chart below to write the words you circled that match the letter patterns for long **u** in each column.

blue	flute	soon	grew
17. _____	18. _____	20. _____	23. _____
	19. _____	21. _____	
		22. _____	

◆ **Directions:** Write the letters on the lines. How many words with the long **u** sound can you make?

s	d	l	b	thr	fl

24. _____ oon   27. _____ ough   28. _____ ew

25. _____ oon   29. _____ ew

26. _____ oon   30. _____ ew

Story Words

◆ **Directions:** Read each word to yourself. Then say the word out loud. Write the word on the line. Check the box after each step.

31. island (is | land)   Read ❑ Say ❑ Write ❑   _____

32. nocturnal   Read ❑ Say ❑ Write ❑   _____
    (noc | tur | nal)

33. carnivore   Read ❑ Say ❑ Write ❑   _____
    (car | ni | vore)

34. marsupial   Read ❑ Say ❑ Write ❑   _____
    (mar | su | pi | al)

35. pouch   Read ❑ Say ❑ Write ❑   _____

36. develop (de | vel | op) Read ❑ Say ❑ Write ❑   _____

Word Bank

Write each of these story words in the Word Bank at the back of this book.

More Word Work

Compound words are made by combining two words. For example, **checkout** and **playground** are compound words.

◆ **Directions:** Write each word as a compound word. Then write it in the sentence.

Example: care + free = carefree

37. blue + print =   _____

    The builder studied the _____.

38. spot + light =   _____

    Some actors love to be in the _____.

39. side + walk =   _____

    Tom ran along the _____.

> **TIP:** Some compound words are joined with a hyphen, others are not joined at all. **Downgrade, blue-green, rocking horse,** and **earthquake** are compound words.

Use What You Know

This selection is about an animal called the Tasmanian devil. Have you heard of this animal before? What kinds of behavior do you think would earn an animal this kind of name? Write what you think on the lines below.

_____

_____

_____

_____

DEVIL DOWN UNDER

A scream rings through the night. Something is running low to the ground. The dark makes it hard to see. You know the animal is nearby. Then its teeth rip into a dead kangaroo. It doesn't chew and it eats quickly. The animal screams again. Another animal tried to take a piece of its meat. Using its paws, it shovels the food down its own throat. In just a moment or two, the meat disappears. The animal does not care about table manners. What it cares about above all else is food.

This is what nighttime might be like if you were to travel to an island called Tasmania. The island is shaped like a heart and is about 120 miles off the southern coast of Australia. This is where you will find Tasmanian devils. They live among the rain forests and grassy fields. Although there are many on the island, you have to go out at night to find them. Devils are nocturnal, which means that they sleep during the day and awake at night.

Tasmanian devils have not been studied very much, because they are nocturnal and because they spend most of their time alone. They also have a history of not being friendly. Years ago, devils were believed to hunt and eat humans. People hunted and killed devils for rewards. People no longer do this today. We know that devils are not a threat to humans. Their fame for having a bad temper, though, **is well deserved.** Devils are angry, grumpy, mean animals. They make horrible screams to let others know how they feel. Their ears turn bright red. Their whiskers stick straight out, and they show as many of their 42 teeth as they can.

Even though people should not be afraid of devils, they are a threat to each other. Once the babies are on their own, only one out of ten will grow to full size. Accidents and disease are two reasons, but the biggest reason is other devils. For example, if a lot of devils find food, they eat in a frenzy and young devils are often killed in the process. In other cases, they will fight each other to the death. The loser becomes **dinner for the day.**

Physically, Tasmanian devils may not be what you expect. If put on a scale, adult male devils weigh about 15 to 20 pounds. Females weigh 12 to17 pounds. They are about the size of a large house cat. The strength of a devil's jaws is not related to its size. Devils can bite hard. The only other animals that compare in jaw strength are sharks and hyenas. Devils use their jaws to eat meat and crush bones. They are carnivores, which means they prefer to eat meat.

To survive, devils must be able to hide and to find their food. They need to do this quickly. Devils eat just about any kind of meat. They also eat a lot. Devils can eat five, ten, or fifteen times their body weight per meal. For a person who weighs 100 pounds, this amount is like eating 500 to 1,500 pounds of food for a lunch. Devils can eat things that would kill other animals. It has been reported that devils can eat some poisons, such as rat poison, and not even get sick.

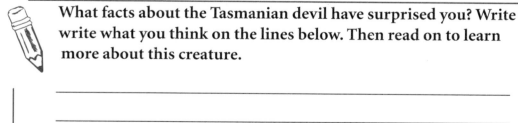

What facts about the Tasmanian devil have surprised you? Write write what you think on the lines below. Then read on to learn more about this creature.

_____

_____

_____

_____

Tasmanian devils are part of a group of animals called marsupials. Marsupials are animals with a pouch. Kangaroos and koalas are also marsupials. These animals give birth when their young are only partly developed. The young animal then develops or grows inside the pouch for a period of time. It is often said that devils are born twice.

The first birth is usually in April or May. It happens in the fall season in Australia and after the mother has been pregnant for three weeks. The babies are about the size of a grain of rice and are partly developed. As many as fifty babies are born at a time, but only four will live. In the race to survive, the babies crawl three inches. The first four that find their mother's nipple will live. These four drink milk and are attached to the mother for 100 days.

The second birth is at three months, when they crawl out of the pouch. At this point, the baby devils have grown fur, so it becomes too warm inside. This usually occurs in early September, the beginning of spring in Australia. Devils spend 15 weeks living in a nest of grasses and leaves. When the mother is not hunting, she returns to the nest to feed the babies and keep them warm. At this point, they are about the size of a newborn puppy. They weigh about half a pound and are three inches long. As they grow bigger, they hunt with their mothers. At first, they hold on to the hair on their mother's back and **catch a ride.** When they have grown larger, they run alongside her.

In November and December, when it is late spring and early summer in Australia, the babies weigh about a pound. They are ready to leave the nest to find homes of their own.

Although hunters nearly killed off all the devils, Australia now has laws to protect them. If you would like to see Tasmanian devils in their natural habitat, you can travel to the land Down Under.

◆

You Be the Judge

◆ 1. Do you think this animal has earned the name "devil"? Why or why not? Write what you think on the lines below.

_____

_____

Think About the Story

Use Story Words

◆ **Directions:** Look at your list of story words on page 46. Write a story word on each line.

2. Animals that give birth to partly developed babies are called _____.

3. Tasmanian devils live on an _____ called Tasmania.

4. _____ animals stay awake at night.

5. Baby devils _____ in the mother's pouch.

6. Another word for meat eater is _____.

7. All marsupials have a _____.

What Are the Facts?

◆ 8. What is true about the Tasmanian devil? Circle the facts.

    a. They can eat ten times their body weight in one meal.

    b. They are friendly to other animals.

    c. They lay eggs.

    d. They hunt at night.

    e. They like to eat plants.

What Can You Tell?

◆ 9. How come people were afraid of the Tasmanian devil for so many years? Explain.

_____

_____

Words and Meanings

◆ **Directions:** Think about how the **bold** words are used in the story. Then circle the words that show the meaning of each word or phrase.

10. The Tasmanian devil's fame for having a bad temper **is well deserved.** This means devils are _____.
    a. friendly animals
    b. nasty, angry, and aggressive
    c. quiet

11. When devils fight, the loser becomes **dinner for the day.** What does this mean?
    a. The devil who loses is eaten.
    b. That devil has to catch the food.
    c. The devil who loses runs away.

12. When the babies get bigger they **catch a ride** on their mother's back. This means that _____.
    a. the babies play catch with stones
    b. the babies learn how to fish
    c. the mother carries the babies

Write Sentences About the Story

◆ **Directions:** Use words from the story to answer these questions.

13. Where do the Tasmanian devils live?

_____

_____

14. What does the Tasmanian devil do during the day?

_____

_____

15. Where does the baby Tasmanian devil live after the first birth? For how long?

_____

_____

16. Where does the baby Tasmanian devil live after the second birth? For how long?

_____

_____

Letters and Sounds

 Directions: The following words have the **c** sound. Circle the words that have the hard **c** sound. Underline the words that have the soft **c** sound.

1. can   2. scene   3. crack   4. comb

> **TIPS:** ▶ A hard **c** sounds like **k,** as in **cop.**
>
> ▶ A soft **c** can be silent, as in **scent,** or it can make an **s** sound, as in **cent.**

 Directions: These words have the **g** sound. Circle the words that have the hard **g** sound. Underline the words that have the soft **g** sound.

5. gate   6. frog   7. through   8. high

> **TIPS:** ▶ A hard **g** sounds like the **g** in **gold.**
>
> ▶ A soft **g** can be silent, as in **bright,** or make a **j** sound, as in **gem.**

Directions: Write each word in the box where it belongs.

cell	pig	corn	grab
fight	science	could	digger
scissors	thigh	gentle	large

hard *c*	soft *c*	hard *g*	soft *g*
9. _____	11. _____	14. _____	17. _____
10. _____	12. _____	15. _____	18. _____
	13. _____	16. _____	19. _____
			20. _____

Directions: Write the letters on the lines. How many words can you make?

| pl | g | b | c | th | r | tr |

21. _____ ain   25. _____ ug   29. _____ ough

22. _____ ain   26. _____ ug   30. _____ ough

23. _____ ain   27. _____ ug   31. _____ ough

24. _____ ain   28. _____ ug   32. _____ ace

33. _____ ace

34. _____ ace

Story Words

Word Bank

Write each of these story words in the Word Bank at the back of this book.

◆ **Directions:** Read each word to yourself. Then say the word out loud. Write the word on the line. Check the box after each step.

35. difference   Read ❑ Say ❑ Write ❑   _____
     (dif | fer | ence)

36. ambassador   Read ❑ Say ❑ Write ❑   _____
     (am | bas | sa | dor)

37. goodwill (good | will) Read ❑ Say ❑ Write ❑   _____

38. humanitarian   Read ❑ Say ❑ Write ❑   _____
     (hu | man | i | tar | i | an)

39. volunteer   Read ❑ Say ❑ Write ❑   _____
     (vol | un | teer)

40. supplies (sup | plies)   Read ❑ Say ❑ Write ❑   _____

More Word Work

You can add prefixes to words. Do this to change the meaning or to make a new word. Prefixes are added to the beginning. For example, the prefix **un** added to the word **done** makes the word **undone.**

◆ **Directions:** Add the prefix to each word. Then write the new word on the line.

Example: un + happy = *unhappy*

41. dis   +   lodge   =   _____

42. re   +   run   =   _____

43. un   +   zip   =   _____

44. pre   +   school   =   _____

45. re   +   heat   =   _____

46. dis   +   comfort =   _____

▶ **TIP:** Different prefixes have different meanings. **Un** and **dis** mean "not," **pre** means "before," and **re** means "again."

Use What You Know

In this selection you will read about a group of people called Airline Ambassadors. They are volunteers who help people in other countries. Have you ever volunteered for something? How have you helped someone else? Write about it on the lines below.

_____

_____

_____

_____

MAKING A DIFFERENCE: AIRLINE AMBASSADORS

Perhaps you have heard this idea before: "Make a difference." You may have also heard that one person can make a difference. Nancy Rivard and the group she started in 1997 is doing just that.

Rivard is a flight attendant for an airline. She has traveled all over the world. Through her travels she began to look at the world as one community. She began to see how people are connected to one another. She was upset when she saw how some children suffer. Rivard thought it might be possible to make a difference. She started Airline Ambassadors International, or "AAI." AAI is delivering goodwill to many people the world over. Goodwill is an act of kindness done without asking for anything in return.

Airline Ambassadors has four different programs: Humanitarian Missions, Youth Programs, Children's Escort Program, and a program of participation in special events and conferences. By January of 2001, AAI had 2,000 volunteers. Each volunteer is good at different things, so they must be matched with jobs that will use their special talents.

To date, AAI has sent humanitarian aid to 22 countries. AAI invites people to use their free time to deliver help to people. The aid may be medicine, medical supplies, food, clothing, toys, or school supplies. Volunteers fly for a lower price on airlines. They take the aid and deliver it. This aid is **worth its weight in gold** to the people who need it.

For example, a team of nine Airline Ambassadors recently carried out a mission to Bolivia. They visited hospitals and delivered 11 wheelchairs, 25 boxes of medical and dental supplies, walkers, canes, stoves, and blankets. All of these materials were badly needed in Bolivia.

Two volunteers raised money before the trip. They knew that many parents in Bolivia did not have the money to pay for their children's hospital care. They planned a golf fund-raiser in Grand Rapids, Michigan. They used the money they raised to help eight children receive medical care and operations.

Another team visited Guatemala. The trip was long and took a lot of effort. Two volunteers had to carry the aid through the mountains on foot. They brought seeds, clothing, and supplies to a small village. The village is made up of people who had to move from their homeland. They had planted a crop of corn, but storms destroyed the crop. Without the seeds, the people would be unable to plant for the season. The Guatemalan people would have no food. The volunteers also gave away airline sweaters. The children were pleased at what the volunteers had done.

Airline Ambassadors also sent a team of 15 volunteers to the Philippines. They threw an early Christmas party at a children's home. Children who do not have parents to raise and care for them live at the home. The volunteers put up a Christmas tree, gave gifts, listened to music, and **had some not-so-quiet fun.** They also raised $7,000 to buy mattresses and sheets for 69 children. Before the volunteers helped, the children had been sleeping on cement blocks, which is like sleeping on flat stones.

Airline Ambassadors' Youth Program volunteers make visits to schools. They talk to students about their work. They explain what AAI does and how the students themselves can make a difference. Many students in the United States have gone on to write letters to children in other countries. They have worked to get supplies and raise money for needy children. Some young volunteers have even gotten to fly on AAI missions and deliver aid to people. The Youth Program also runs an art contest. They invite children to draw pictures about global problems and issues. As of the year 2000, 62,000 children in 54 countries have entered the contest.

> **Do you think you would like to work with AAI in any way? Why or why not? Write what you think on the lines below. Then keep reading to find out more.**
>
> _____
>
> _____
>
> _____
>
> _____

The Children's Escort Program helps children travel. Volunteers who work for the airlines fly with children. For example, Masako Fett has escorted many children. In September of 2000, she flew to Moscow to pick up a six-year-old who was born without a leg. This child needs to fly to the United States once a year for medical treatment. Masako kept the child company and helped her get to Seattle.

AAI has also helped children who are coming to live in the United States. In November 2000, they helped five Ethiopian children travel to new homes where they are being adopted.

Airline Ambassadors participate in many special events and conferences. They have local chapters in 15 different American cities. They also have programs in other countries. AAI has volunteers that help with local needs. These can include repainting a local school or helping children at a Special Olympics event. Members of AAI work as volunteers at international events, such as the Prayer Vigil for the Earth in Washington, D.C., and the Global Summit on Peace in Jordan. AAI is **trying to build on** the goodwill work already done by the airlines and volunteers.

AAI has helped many people in its four years of existence. Because of the hard work and service of its volunteers, they are making a difference.

You Be the Judge

◆ 1. Of the four AAI programs, which do you think helps the most? Explain. Write what you think on the lines below.

_____

_____

2. AAI has done a lot in four years. What do you think will happen to the organization in the future? Write what you think on the lines below.

_____

_____

Think About the Story

Use Story Words

◆ **Directions:** Look at your list of story words on page 53. Write a story word on each line.

3. A _____ is someone who works without pay.

4. Many types of _____ are moved by airplanes.

5. Airline _____ is the name of this group.

6. The people of AAI try to build _____.

7. The program called _____ Missions delivers aid to people.

8. Everyone helps make a _____.

Write Sentences About the Story

◆ **Directions:** Use words from the story to answer these questions.

9. What is the goal of the Airline Ambassadors International?

_____

10. What do volunteers do that are sent on AAI humanitarian missions? Give one specific answer.

_____

_____

11. What do volunteers in AAI's Youth Program do?

_____

_____

What Are the Facts?

◈ **Directions:** Write **T** next to the sentences that say true things about the story. Write **F** next to the sentences that do not.

12. _____ Nancy Rivard started AAI in 1982.

13. _____ AAI has helped many children.

14. _____ Every volunteer is paid for the work that they do.

15. _____ Wheelchairs were given to people in Bolivia.

Words and Meanings

◈ **Directions:** Think about how the bold words are used in the story. Then circle the words that show the meaning of each word or phrase.

16. The aid is **worth its weight in gold** to the people who need it. This means that _____.
    a. people gave gold for aid
    b. aid is very important
    c. the aid is not worth much

17. The volunteers gave a party and **had some not-so-quiet fun.** What did this mean?
    a. The party was boring.
    b. The kids did not like the party.
    c. The party was loud.

18. AAI is **trying to build on** the work already done. This means that _____.
    a. they would like to do more
    b. they feel they have done enough for others
    c. they will do no more volunteer work

Why Did It Happen?

◈ **Directions:** Draw a line to match the cause to the effect.

19. AAI gave seeds.   ○ Eight children receive medical help.

20. AAI visits American schools.   ○ Children have beds to sleep on.

21. Volunteers raise money.   ○ Food is planted for the growing season.

22. Volunteers buy mattresses.   ○ Students learn how they can help.

Chapter 1 Summary of Skills and Strategies

Let's look back at what you learned in Chapter 1.

Letters and Sounds

◆ You learned that. . .

- letter patterns can help you know if a word has a long or a short vowel sound.
- many different letter groups can stand for a long vowel sound.
- the letters **ay** and **eigh** can sound like the vowel sound in **stay.**
- the letters **y** and **ie** can sound like the vowel sound in **try.**
- when vowels are combined they sound differently.
- the letters **c** and **g** can be both hard and soft, as in the words **can** and **high.**

Stories and Skills

◆ You learned about. . .

- characters who solve problems and accept responsibilities.
- an explorer, a plane full of scientists, and an organization of volunteers who make the world better for others.
- an animal that has his eye on only one thing—the next meal.

◆ You learned. . .

- how to use what you know to help you understand stories.
- how to look ahead, or predict, what story characters might do.

Words and Meanings

◆ You learned. . .

- how to add endings and beginnings to words.
- how to make words plural.
- how to use **'s** and **s'** to show that something belongs to someone.
- how to make compound words.

The chapter review will give you a chance to show what you have learned.

Part A

Summing It Up: Letters and Sounds

▸ The letter **y** can be any vowel sound, such as the short **i** in **gym**.

▸ When vowels are combined, as in **bread** or **young**, they may have the sound of one of the vowels.

Directions: Write each word that belongs in the list.

sit	tread	led	bread
build	brought	crystal	fought

short *e*	short *i*	short *o*
1. _____	4. _____	7. _____
2. _____	5. _____	8. _____
3. _____	6. _____	

▸ The letters **e, ee, ea, ey,** and **y** can sound like the long **e** sound.

▸ The letters **a, ai , ay, ei, ea, eigh,** and **ey** can sound like the long **a** sound.

Directions: Put a box around all the words that have the long **e** sound. Underline the words that have the long **a** sound. Circle the letter or letters that stand for the long **e** or the long **a** sound

9. wake	12. seed	15. grape	18. achieve
10. trip	13. said	16. bee	19. monkey
11. treat	14. away	17. sleigh	20. wait

▸ The letters **igh, y, i, ie,** and **e-e** can all stand for the long **i** sound.

▸ The letters **oa, ow, o, oe,** and **ough** can all stand for the long **o** sound.

▸ The letters **u, ue, oo, ui, ew, ou,** and **ough** can all stand for the long **u** sound.

◆ **Directions:** Write each word below in the list where it belongs.

boat	through	throw	radio
nice	fly	new	soon
blue	phone	might	pie

long *o*	long *i*	long *u*
21. _____	25. _____	29. _____
22. _____	26. _____	30. _____
23. _____	27. _____	31. _____
24. _____	28. _____	32. _____

▸ The letter **c** can have a hard sound, as in the word **can**, or a soft sound, as in the word **scene**.

▸ The letter **g** can have a hard sound, as in the word **great**, or a soft sound, as in the word **height**.

◆ **Directions:** Write each word below in the list where it belongs.

cone	right	sight	fig
scent	tag	cat	corn
grape	science	trough	

hard *c*	soft *c*	hard *g*	soft *g*
33. _____	36. _____	38. _____	41. _____
34. _____	37. _____	39. _____	42. _____
35. _____		40. _____	43. _____

Part B

Summing It Up: More Word Work

> ▸ You can add the endings **ed** and **ing** to verbs.
>
> ▸ Add **ed** to make a verb tell about the past.
>
> ▸ Add **ing** to make a verb tell about the present or future.

Directions: Add **ed** or **ing** to each word below to finish the sentence.

1. go   Michael is _____ to the store this afternoon.

2. spot   Riley _____ the dog running loose yesterday.

3. wait   Mrs. Smith _____ after school for her children.

4. brush   Ling is _____ her hair.

> ▸ To make a word plural, or mean more than one, add an **s** or **es**.
>
> ▸ If a word ends in **sh, z, x,** or **ch,** add **es**.
>
> ▸ If a word ends in **f,** change it to a **v** before adding **s** or **es**.
>
> ▸ If a word ends in **y,** change it to an **i,** then add **es**.
>
> ▸ Irregular plurals have different spellings. For example, **goose** becomes **geese** and **woman** becomes **women**.

Directions: Make each word plural. Write it on the line.

5. wish _____

6. horse _____

7. hat _____

8. life _____

9. penny _____

10. child _____

11. class _____

12. box _____

▲ ▶ You can add prefixes to the beginnings of words to change their meanings.

▶ Add **un** or **dis** to make a word mean "not" something, as in the word **unzip.**

▶ Add **re** to make a word mean "again," as in the word **rerun.**

▶ Add **pre** to make a word mean "before" something, as in the word **preheat.**

Directions: Add the prefix to each word. Write the new word in the sentence.

13. **un** + do   "I'm trying to _____ this button," said Sally.

14. **pre** + school   There are 14 children in the _____ class.

15. **re** + heated   The food was _____.

16. **dis** + agreement The brothers were having a _____.

▲ ▶ You can add **'s** or **s'** to show ownership.

▶ Add **'s** to most nouns.

▶ Add only the **'** to plural nouns ending in **s,** as in **the three doctors' nurse.**

Directions: Make each word below show ownership by adding **'s, s',** or **'.** Write it on the line to complete the sentence.

17. Jose   _____ sister is in my math class.

18. clerks   The four _____ calculators are not working today.

19. Mr. Simon That is _____ car.

▲ ▶ Compound words are two words joined together to form new words.

Directions: In the list of words below, draw a line between the two words. Write the two words on the lines.

20. uptown   _____   22. gentleman _____

21. watermelon _____   23. daydream _____

Part C

Story Words

◆ **Directions:** Write the word from the list that matches each clue.

| idea | algebra | develop | fine | supplies |

1. to grow _____

2. a type of math _____

3. things you need _____

4. things are okay _____

5. something you think of _____

◆ **Directions:** On the lines below, write a word from the list to finish each sentence.

| nocturnal | volunteer | explore | intensify | cafeteria |

6. John Muir liked to _____ the mountains and countryside.

7. Animals that are active only at night are _____.

8. If a hurricane were to _____ it might do more damage.

9. Food is served in a _____.

10. A person who works without pay is a _____.

◆ **Directions:** Read each word. On the lines below, write a number to tell how many syllables the word has.

11. marsupial _____   13. ambassador _____

12. preserve _____   14. session _____

◆ **Directions:** Write the word from the list that matches each clue.

| carnivore | reservoir | kennel | journal | pamphlet |

15. like a diary _____

16. a metal cage _____

17. an animal that eats meat _____

18. information printed on pages _____

19. lake that holds water _____

◆ **Directions:** Write a word from the list to finish each sentence.

island	shelters	preserve
seriously	nature	difference

20. Airline Ambassadors is making a _____ to children around the world.

21. Muir worked to _____ Yosemite.

22. Tasmania is an _____ located near Australia.

23. Stray dogs and cats are often put into animal _____.

24. Some people take themselves too _____.

25. If you like to hike, you probably like _____.

Part D

Think About the Stories

Who Did What?

◆ **Directions:** Read this list from the stories you read in Chapter 1. Write a name to answer each question.

Buck	Julie	Riley	Luis
Brad	John Muir	Nancy Rivard	

1. Who likes to write in a journal? _____

2. Who met with President Roosevelt to create the National Park System? _____

3. Who is an expert on training dogs? _____

4. Who founded an organization that brings supplies to needy children? _____

5. Who hung up posters to find Flip-Flop? _____

6. Who helps Luis make his dog posters? _____

7. Who told Luis to wake up in class? _____

Why Did It Happen?

◆ **Directions:** Read each event. Circle the reasons why.

8. Luis hung up posters with Flip-Flop's picture on them.
    a. Luis was worried about Flip-Flop.
    b. Luis wanted to show everyone his dog.
    c. Luis thought this would be a good way to find Flip-Flop.

9. John Muir wrote many articles and books about nature.
    a. Muir wanted people to take care of the environment.
    b. Muir wanted to share his love of nature.
    c. Muir wanted to meet the President.

Think About Details

◆ **Directions:** Each detail below comes from a story in Chapter 1. Write the details next to the stories they go with.

| juice boxes | circular storm | boxes of medicine |
| half-eaten sneaker | carried in a pouch | carriage repair shop |

10. "Dear Journal" _____

11. "John Muir: The Father of Our National Parks"

    _____

12. "Devil Down Under" _____

13. "Making a Difference: Airline Ambassadors"

    _____

14. "Into the Eye" _____

15. "Flip-Flop: A Fine Dog" _____

CHAPTER 2

▶ **Lesson 1** . . . . *page 68*
    "Double Trouble," Part 1

▶ **Lesson 2** . . . . *page 75*
    "Double Trouble," Part 2

▶ **Lesson 3** . . . . *page 82*
    "Book Talk"

▶ **Lesson 4** . . . . *page 89*
    "Out of This World Research," Part 1

▶ **Lesson 5** . . . . *page 96*
    "Out of This World Research," Part 2

▶ **Lesson 6** . . . . *page 103*
    "Slam Dunk"

▶ **Lesson 7** . . . . *page 110*
    "As Far As the Eye Can See"

Letters and Sounds

◆ **Directions:** These words have the **f** sound. Circle the letters that make the **f** sound in each word.

1. cough
2. graph
3. tough
4. phonic

> **TIP:** The letters **ph,** as in **nephew,** and **gh,** as in **cough,** can make the **f** sound.

◆ **Directions:** Read these words. Circle each one that has the **f** sound.

5. basket	9. class	13. chalk	16. telephone
6. phony	10. rhyme	14. chair	17. laugh
7. sulphur	11. rough	15. enough	18. cough
8. photo	12. marked		

◆ **Directions:** Write the letters on the lines. How many words can you make?

en	l	r	gr	c	t

19. _____ ough   23. _____ augh

20. _____ ough

21. _____ ough   24. _____ aph

22. _____ ough

Story Words

Word Bank

Write each of these story words in the Word Bank at the back of this book.

◆ **Directions:** Read each word to yourself. Then say the word out loud. Write the word on the line. Check the box after each step.

25. blouse   Read ❑ Say ❑ Write ❑ _____

26. whirling (whirl│ing) Read ❑ Say ❑ Write ❑ _____

27. twins   Read ❑ Say ❑ Write ❑ _____

28. double (dou│ble)   Read ❑ Say ❑ Write ❑ _____

29. number (num│ber)   Read ❑ Say ❑ Write ❑ _____

30. textbook   Read ❑ Say ❑ Write ❑ _____
     (text│book)

31. sternly (stern│ly)   Read ❑ Say ❑ Write ❑ _____

More Word Work

To compare two or more things, add the suffix **er** to make a word mean "more." Add the suffix **est** to make a word mean "the most."

Example: Jamal thinks basketball is an easy sport to play.
                Jamal thinks basketball is easier to play than baseball.
                Jamal thinks basketball is the easiest sport to play.

◆ **Directions:** To make each word mean "more," add **er.** Then write the word in the sentence.

Example: hot hotter → Summer is hotter than winter.

32. happy _____ → A dog that is walked is _____
                             than a dog that is not.

33. cold   _____ → Today is _____ than yesterday.

> **TIP:** When adding **er** or **est** to words that end in **y,** change the **y** to an **i,** then add **er.** For example: **er** added to **happy** becomes **happier,** not **happyer.**

◆ **Directions:** Make each word mean "the most." Add **est.** Then write each word in a sentence.

34. happy _____ → _____
                       _____.

35. cold   _____ → _____
                       _____.

Use What You Know

Robby is babysitting for the first time. What are some important things that you think a babysitter should know? Write about them on the lines below.

_____

_____

_____

_____

DOUBLE TROUBLE, PART 1

Robby stood in the middle of the entryway and clutched the note in his hand. He opened and read it one more time, just to make sure he was at the right apartment. After a deep breath, he knocked gently on the door. He thought he heard screaming and then running feet on the other side. "I'm not sure if I'm **cut out for this job,**" he thought, "I've never done this before. But, how hard can it be to take care of a couple of kids?"

A woman with dark brown hair and kind eyes answered the door. She was dressed in navy pants and a nice blouse. She smiled. "You must be Robby. Your mother has told me a lot about you. Please come in. Boys, come here and meet Robby," she called.

After a moment, Robby finally said, "You must be Mrs. Johnson."

"Yes, and—Boys!" Mrs. Johnson said looking over her shoulder.

Just then, two identical red-headed boys with glasses came whirling around the corner and latched on to their mother's legs. They hid behind her and peeked out from behind to look up at Robby. "They are shy at first, but the twins will warm up to you in no time," Mrs. Johnson explained. "This one is Alex and this one is Aidan."

"Hello Alex and Aidan," said Robby squatting down so he was about the same height. "My name is Robby. I feel like I'm seeing double. How old are you guys?"

Alex stuck out four fingers and Aidain held up five. Then they both counted, "one, two, three, four."

The boys giggled and ran off to the living room. Robby followed Mrs. Johnson into the kitchen. "Here's the number at my office, Mr. Johnson's phone number, and our emergency numbers. There are snacks in the cupboard. I'd prefer the boys not to have any treats until after their dinner. You can fix them macaroni and cheese, carrots, and milk for dinner. Help yourself. I have to get to work now, but Mr. Johnson should be home no later than seven. Have fun."

After Mrs. Johnson left, Robby set his backpack up on the kitchen table. He pulled out his World History textbook and flipped to Chapter 3. He sat down and looked over the material for the next day's quiz. "The boys are playing, and I'll make them a snack in a few minutes," he thought. "They seem shy. Maybe I should just let them come to me when they are ready." After a while he realized it was quiet, very quiet. "I wonder what they are doing," he asked himself.

Robby went into the living room. He thought the boys were there since they had just been building with blocks. A pirate ship complete with a paper sail sat on the floor, along with coloring books, markers, black and red checker pieces, and a stuffed bear. Robby tip-toed around the toys and walked down the hall to the bedrooms thinking one question. "How could I have lost them already?" he thought. "Maybe they are just playing hide and seek."

"Someone is hiding, where are you?" Robby called out. The twins didn't answer him. Robby checked under the boys' beds and then in the closet. Robby began to speed up the search. He ran back to the living room and checked behind the sofa. All he found was the cat, **curled up like a ball,** on the heating vent. Robby's stomach churned as he searched. "This is just great. Five minutes on the job as a babysitter, and I don't even know where the kids are. Enough of this!" Then he heard some shuffling. It came from Mr. and Mrs. Johnson's bedroom.

He twisted the door knob, but the boys had locked it. He jiggled harder, but it wouldn't open. "Come on guys, open up," Robby said.

"It wasn't me. Aidan locked the door," Alex said.

"Did not!" Aidan wailed.

"Did too!"

"Just open the door," Robby said.

"You gotta use the screwdriver. Momma pokes it in the hole."

"Where's the screwdriver?" Robby asked, beginning to sweat.

"There!" yelled the boys through the door.

 If you were Robby, would you feel nervous? Circle your answer.

YES   NO

Then keep reading to find out what takes place.

Robby wasn't sure where to find the screwdriver. His eyes darted from place to place and then out of the corner of his eye, he spied something. He reached up and pulled a screwdriver from the top of the frame. He shoved the end in the hole and twisted the knob. The door swung open. Robby was relieved to see the boys were okay. Then he looked around the bedroom. It was the biggest mess he had ever seen!

"What happened in here?"

"It was his idea," Aidan said tartly.

"Was not."

"Was too!" Aidan said, leaning his face close to his brother's.

"Knock it off you two," Robby said sternly. "Alex you get the wastebasket. Aidan, start picking this paper up."

"I'm not Aidan, he is."

"Whichever one you are, we've got to clean this mess up. NOW," Robby said, his head beginning to feel **like a train wreck.**

The boys stopped talking right away. They stared at Robby with their feet glued to the floor that looked like a sea of paper. Robby asked, "How much paper did you guys unroll?"

"Uh, I don't know," Alex said.

After the Johnson's bedroom was cleaned up, Robby emptied the wastebasket into a larger trash bag. He would take it out to the trash. Robby didn't want Mrs. Johnson to think he had done a bad job on his first day. Robby also decided he wouldn't leave the boys **to their own devices** anymore. Even so, Robby wondered if this was the right job for him. He could hardly wait for Mr. Johnson to come home. This was rough. ▶

You Be the Judge

◆ **1.** How do you think Robby handled his first day on the job? Write what you think on the lines below.

_____

_____

Think About the Story

Use Story Words

◆ **Directions:** Look at your list of story words on page 69. Write a story word on each line.

2. To make a _____ batch of cookies, use twice the amount of ingredients.

3. Two babies born at the same time are _____.

4. John put a cover on his math _____.

5. When a top spins round and round it is _____.

6. Robby spoke _____ because he wanted the boys to listen.

7. The red _____ matches Eva's favorite skirt.

8. She gave him her phone _____.

Write Sentences About the Story

◆ **Directions:** Read each sentence. Circle the word that best fits in each sentence. Then write the sentence on the line.

9. I (am/be) somewhat nervous.

_____

_____

10. Alex and Aidan (will be/seem) to have a lot of energy.

_____

_____

11. Mrs. Johnson (will be/get) upset if the boys misbehave.

_____

_____

What Can You Tell?

12. How did Robby handle the boys at the beginning of the afternoon? How did it compare to later after he had spent a little time with them? Write what you think on the lines below.

_____

_____

Words and Meanings

◆ **Directions:** Think about how the **bold** words are used in the story. Then circle the words that show the meaning of each word or phrase.

13. Robby was not sure if he was **"cut out for this job."** This means that _____.
    a. Robby had babysat many times before
    b. Robby was feeling nervous
    c. he cut an add out of the paper for the job

14. The cat was **curled up like a ball.** What did this mean?
    a. The cat had its legs pulled in close.
    b. The cat was rolling around.
    c. The cat liked to play with balls.

15. At one point Robby's head felt **like a train wreck.** What did this mean?
    a. The boys were playing with trains.
    b. Robby wrecked the toy trains.
    c. Robby had a headache.

16. Robby also decided he wouldn't leave the boys **to their own devices** anymore. This means that _____.
    a. Robby planned to watch the boys carefully
    b. he was going to let the boys play outside by themselves
    c. Robby was going to help the boys make a mess in the kitchen

Look Ahead

◆ 17. How do you think Robby will get along with the boys? What do you think might happen? Write your thoughts on the lines below. Read on to find out if you are right.

_____

_____

Letters and Sounds

◆ **Directions:** These words have the schwa sound **en.** Circle the letters that make the **schwa** sound.

1. station   2. listen   3. ration   4. fraction

> **TIP:** Vowels that make a **schwa** sound are called weak stress vowels. The letters **io** in **lotion** make the **schwa** sound **en.** This sound can be spelled **ion** or **en.**

◆ **Directions:** Read these words. Circle each one that has the **schwa** sound **en.**

5. motion	8. spike	11. bowl	14. ration
6. plant	9. tools	12. potion	15. cheer
7. silent	10. talent	13. stationery	16. apple

◆ **Directions:** Read these words. Write each word under the matching silent letter.

wheel	white	column	often
listen	night	fright	stretched

silent *t*	silent *h*	silent *n*
17. _____	20. _____	24. _____
18. _____	21. _____	
19. _____	22. _____	
	23. _____	

> **TIP:** Some consonants such as **t, h,** and **n** can be silent. For example, when you say the word **right,** you do not hear the **h** sound.

Story Words

◆ **Directions:** Read each word to yourself. Then say the word out loud. Write the word on the line. Check the box after each step.

25. thought   Read ❑ Say ❑ Write ❑ _____

26. listen (lis | ten)   Read ❑ Say ❑ Write ❑ _____

27. continent   Read ❑ Say ❑ Write ❑ _____
    (con | ti | nent)

28. climb   Read ❑ Say ❑ Write ❑ _____

29. spiral (spi | ral)   Read ❑ Say ❑ Write ❑ _____

Word Bank

Write each of these story words in the Word Bank at the back of this book.

More Word Work

As you know, you can add **'s** to show that a thing belongs to someone or has a connection to someone. This is called the possessive form.

◆ **Directions:** Add **'s** to each word to make it possessive. For words that already end in **s,** just add **'**.

Example: Lisa   Lisa's → Here is Lisa's house.

30. Emilio _____ → These are _____ keys.

31. students _____ → The _____ tests are all graded.

32. dog _____ → The _____ bone is on the ground.

33. parents _____ → All of the _____ expressions were happy.

Use What You Know

In Part 2 of this story Robby has returned to babysit for Alex and Aidan. He is not sure of how things will go. Have you ever had a job that you felt unsure of? How did you handle it? Write about it on the lines below.

_____

_____

_____

_____

DOUBLE TROUBLE, PART 2

Robby tried to smile at Mrs. Johnson. He thought, "I can't believe I came back for another day of this. I hope the boys listen to me this time. Yesterday was a disaster. Maybe they will behave today."

"Welcome back Robby. I'm so glad you're here. You know good babysitters are hard to find," she went on. "And we have sampled our share. Haven't we boys?"

"Robby's here! Robby's here!" the boys chanted in the living room. It sounded like a weird melody.

For a fraction of a second, Robby thought about turning around and running as fast as he could. He saw himself bolting like lightning, but for some reason he didn't move.

After Mrs. Johnson left for work Robby called, "Boys it's time for a snack."

Aidan and Alex ran into the kitchen.

"How would you guys like some apples?" Robby asked, as he washed one in the sink. He dried it with a paper towel and set it on a napkin.

"We don't like apples that way," declared Alex.

Robby wasn't sure there was another way to eat an apple, but he asked anyway. "How do you like them?"

"We like them cut up, with no skin," said Alex.

"And we like to eat them in a bowl, with a fork," added Aidan, giggling.

Robby could see that the boys were going to start testing him again. Instead of reacting, he decided to play it cool.

Robby opened the cupboards, both top and bottom. The boys laughed louder. As Robby turned around he saw the boys hiding beneath the table. "Hey what's going on under there?" Robby asked, leaning over at an angle.

Alex and Aidan were trying to hide the fact that they were eating candy. "You know the rules, no candy before dinner. Hand it over," Robby said.

As Robby reached over, the boys shoved as much as they could into their mouths. Rainbow-colored rivers ran down from the corners of their mouths. "Ugh," laughed Robby. This made them laugh even harder.

"Boys, make a trip to the trash can and spit that stuff out. Otherwise, you'll spend the rest of the afternoon sitting in a chair," ordered Robby.

Two sets of eyes stared at him in disbelief.

"I said spit it out."

The boys did as they were told, much to Robby's surprise. The twins became silent. They looked at Robby, trying to figure out what to do next.

Robby prepared the snack and sat down with the boys. Then he saw his World History book. "I really have to study for that quiz," he thought. Robby began reading. Aidan said, "Let me see." Alex cried, "No, let me. LET ME!" Soon the boys were playing tug-of-war with the book.

"Give it back to me," said Robby, taking the book away from them. He showed the boys the map in the front.

"What's this?" Aidan asked, with a mouthful of apple.

"That's the continent of Africa," Robby explained. "There are seven continents." The boys ate and listened while Robby talked about the map. After the snack, Robby had an idea. "Hey boys, let's go on a trip!"

"Really?" the boys asked.

It took a lot longer than Robby expected to get the boys' sneakers and coats on. Alex kept complaining and needed help finding one of his shoes. Once they went outside, the fresh air seemed to be **just what Alex needed.** The boys ran along the sidewalk.

Do you think Robby likes the job more than yesterday? Circle your answer.

YES   NO

Then keep reading to find out what takes place.

"Boys, do you see those four-wheeled monsters?" Robby asked, looking at a line of traffic. "We've got to stay out of their way."

"Daddy says that if we're not careful, we could even get killed by one of those trucks," said Aidan.

"If one runs you over," added Alex.

"That's right, so we'd better watch out," Robby whispered.

At the park, Robby thought the best way to **keep track of** the boys was to keep them busy. They played spacecraft in the wooden fort. Robby had them climb the ladder that seemed **as tall as a skyscraper.** Over and over. They took turns slipping through the hole at the top of the spiral slide. Robby chased the boys and pretended to be an enemy ship.

"Stop," Alex begged.

"Poor Alex," Aidan teased, "You're too much of a baby to keep up."

Robby told them to keep their spacecraft on track, or the enemy would throw them overboard. The boys decided to be quiet.

Robby practically had to drag the boys back to the apartment. While Robby made dinner, the boys watched TV. They seemed worn out from running around so much. They were too tired to come up with any more trouble.

After dinner, Mr. Johnson came home. "Daddy! Daddy!" they yelled.

Mr. Johnson hugged the boys and said, "I hope today was less painful than yesterday Robby. You're our third babysitter this month."

"It wasn't bad at all," Robby heard himself say, "In fact, we had a good time together. Alex and Aidan, I'll see you two tomorrow."

"YEAH!" they yelled, giving Robby a double hug good-bye.

Robby walked home thinking about all the games he would play with the twins tomorrow. He was glad he had stuck it out instead of quitting. This new job was going to work out after all.

You Be the Judge

◆ 1. Do you think taking the boys to the park was a good idea? Why or why not? Write what you think on the lines below.

_____

_____

2. Summarize Robby's second babysitting experience to explain why the twins will look forward to Robby's next visit. Write four sentences explaining what you think on the lines below.

_____

_____

_____

_____

Think About the Story

Use Story Words

◆ **Directions:** Look at your list of story words on page 76. Write a story word on each line.

3. The boys wanted to _____ into the fort.

4. Africa is one of the _____ of the world.

5. Robby _____ the boys deserved a second chance.

6. A _____ slide goes around and down in a circle.

7. Robby wondered if the boys were going to _____ to him.

Write Sentences About the Story

◆ **Directions:** Use words from the story to answer these questions.

8. What does Robby do when the boys start testing him?

_____

_____

9. How does Robby feel about his new job at the end of the day?

_____

_____

What's the Big Idea?

10. Which sentence sums up the most important idea of "Double Trouble," Part 2? Circle the sentence.

    a. Robby took the boys to the park.

    b. Alex and Aidan like to go on the slide.

    c. Robby learned that he could handle being a babysitter.

Words and Meanings

Directions: Think about how the **bold** words are used in the story. Then circle the answer that shows the meaning of each word or phrase.

11. The fresh air seemed to be **just what Alex needed.** This means that _____.

    a. Alex was happier once they were outside

    b. Alex continued to complain

    c. Alex wanted to go back inside

12. At the park Robby did his best to **keep track of** Alex and Aidan. What did this mean?

    a. Robby lost the boys.

    b. Robby made a track in the sand for boys to drive their trucks.

    c. Robby watched out for both boys.

13. To the boys the ladder seemed **as tall as a skyscraper.** This means that _____.

    a. the ladder was tall

    b. the ladder looked like a building

    c. the ladder was in a city

When Did It Happen?

14. Write a number from 1 to 5 in front of each event to show when it happened.

    _____ Robby made the boys spit out the candy.

    _____ The boys ate apples.

    _____ The boys and Robby played games at the park.

    _____ Robby felt good about the job he did.

    _____ Alex couldn't find one of his shoes.

Letters and Sounds

◆ **Directions:** These words have silent consonants. Circle the consonant or consonants that are silent in each word.

    1. gnome   **2.** knee   **3.** high   **4.** comb   **5.** write

> **TIP:** The letters **w, g, k, b,** and **h** can be silent. For example, when you say the word **knee,** you hear the **n** sound. Words like **knee** and **write** have the consonant-consonant-vowel pattern, or CCV.

◆ **Directions:** Read these words. Circle each one that has a silent consonant.

6. light	**9.** gnu	**12.** when	**15.** kite
7. knight	**10.** knot	**13.** class	**16.** gnashing
8. tomb	**11.** claim	**14.** wrestle	**17.** ghost

◆ **Directions:** Write each word you circled under the sound that is silent. You may use the same word more than once.

silent *g*	silent *b*	silent *h*
18. _____	22. _____	23. _____
19. _____		24. _____
20. _____		25. _____
21. _____		26. _____

silent *k*	silent *w*
27. _____	29. _____
28. _____	

> **TIP:** Some words may have more than one silent letter. For example, the letters **g** and **h** are both silent in the word **fright.** You may want to say each word out loud.

Story Words

◆ **Directions:** Read each word to yourself. Then say the word out loud. Write the word on the line. Check the box after each step.

Word Bank

Write each of these story words in the Word Bank at the back of this book.

30. published   Read ❑ Say ❑ Write ❑ _____
    (pub | lish | ed)

31. recommended   Read ❑ Say ❑ Write ❑ _____
    (rec | om | mend | ed)

32. property   Read ❑ Say ❑ Write ❑ _____
    (prop | er | ty)

33. powerful   Read ❑ Say ❑ Write ❑ _____
    (pow | er | ful)

34. scolded (scold | ed)   Read ❑ Say ❑ Write ❑ _____

35. lawyer (law | yer)   Read ❑ Say ❑ Write ❑ _____

36. payment (pay | ment) Read ❑ Say ❑ Write ❑ _____

More Word Work

◆ **Directions:** Rewrite each sentence. Use **'s** or **s'** to show ownership or possession.

Example: The story the book tells is unusual.
               The book's story is unusual.

37. The picture Stacey drew is neat.

   _____

38. The new housepaint the Cervantes used looks nice.

   _____

39. The dog Cassie has likes to dig.

   _____

Use What You Know

Have you ever seen a movie or read a book that you liked enough to tell a friend about? Or, has a friend ever recommended a movie or book to you? Tell about it on the lines below.

_____

_____

_____

_____

BOOK TALK

I pull the thick book off the shelf at the library. It looks like many people before me have read it. I take this as a good sign. I think about where the story will take me. I think about the characters I will meet and the problems they are sure to face. I look at the cover and study the drawing. It is a drawing of a young African-American girl. Her eyes seem to be filled with hope and pride, or maybe surprise. She wears a white dress with a high collar.

The title of the book I'm writing about is *Roll of Thunder, Hear My Cry*. It was written by Mildred D. Taylor and was published in 1976. It was recommended to me by a friend.

First, I will tell you a little about the story. The story is about many things. Most of all it is about the human spirit: the will to take pride in one's self; the energy to take a stand in what one believes in; and last, the strength to always have hope. The story is told through the eyes of Cassie Logan, a girl who is about 8 years old. Cassie and her family live on a farm

in Mississippi. The Logans are unusual because they own their own property. In the South in the 1930s, not many African Americans owned their own land. Many white characters in the story dislike the Logans for this reason. Events that take place in the story may cause them to lose their land. The Logans prove that they will do just about anything to keep their land and hold on to their pride.

The book begins as Cassie and her brothers are walking to school. It is their first day of school. They are not enjoying the hour-long trip to school. Cassie's younger brother, Little Man, is worried about his clothes getting dirty. You see, the road they have to take is a dirt road. The writer does such a good job of describing the scene that I can almost taste the fine red dust in my mouth. I can almost feel the heat of the morning sun beating down on my head. I am surprised by the fact that the first day of school is on an October morning. I find out later that the African-American children have to spend half the year working to farm cotton.

The white students take a bus to school. There are many scenes in the book that describe the buses zooming by Cassie and the others. During the rainy season, the bus forces them to jump off the roadside, into deep water. Then they have to spend the rest of the day caked in mud. One of my favorite parts of the book is where Stacey, Cassie's older brother, forms a plan to fight back. He and a few others dig a trough across the road. After school they lay in the bushes as the rain pours down. The bus cruises by and then gets stuck in the ditch. The children have to jump out in the mud and walk home. Cassie and her brothers watch **with satisfaction.**

Later that night a neighbor knocks on the door. He warns them to take care because some people are "out riding." I learn that this means that there is an angry group of prejudiced men out looking for a fight. Stacey and Cassie are scared that their Mama will find out what they have done. They are nervous that they may have started something they can't stop.

One of the most powerful scenes in the book is when Cassie goes with her mother to town. Cassie goes into a store with her brother and friend. She gets very upset and can't understand why the white customers are treated differently. She tells the storekeeper how she feels. Then Cassie is scolded by him and kicked out. The trouble continues out on the street when she bumps into a white girl. The father of the girl yells at Cassie and then pushes her off the sidewalk. After all this abuse, Cassie is forced to say she is sorry. As I read this part of the story, I felt as if a part of Cassie's spirit died also.

Later Cassie's Papa tells her, "Cassie, there'll be a whole lot of things you ain't gonna wanna do, but you'll have to do in this life just so you can survive. . . . But there are other things, Cassie, that if I'd let be, they'd eat away at me and destroy me in the end. And it's the same with you, Baby. There are things you can't back down on, things you gotta **take a stand on.** But it's up to you to decide what they are."

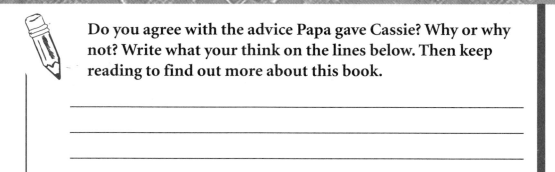

Do you agree with the advice Papa gave Cassie? Why or why not? Write what your think on the lines below. Then keep reading to find out more about this book.

_____

_____

_____

_____

Later in the book Cassie uses her wit and nerve to make the girl understand how she feels.

The tension continues to rise as the Logans try to get their neighbors to stop shopping at the Wallaces' store. The Wallaces go "out riding" regularly and believe that things should remain as they were before the War Between the States. The Logans **iron out a deal** with a white lawyer from another town. The Wallaces and their friends are not exactly pleased about losing business. They are also upset about the Logans taking a stand. They threaten Cassie's family.

Papa, Stacey, and Mr. Morrison, who is a worker on the farm, go on a shopping trip. On the way home the Wallaces attack them. Papa gets a gunshot wound, and then the wagon rolls over his leg and breaks it. Mr. Morrison fights the other men and scares them away.

The injury forces Papa to stay home. He cannot return to work. Money is so **scarce** that they have a hard time making their payment for the land. Help from a family member and their belief in themselves are the only things that get them through.

I'm not going to tell you how the story ends. All I can say is that Papa finds a way for everyone to work together on something.

If you have the chance, pick up _Roll of Thunder, Hear My Cry_. When I began reading, the hardest part was the Southern talk. It was as hard as reading French. Once I got used to it, though, Cassie's voice pulled me into the story. She and her family taught me something about pride, courage, and hope.

◆

You Be the Judge

◆ 1. Do you think *Roll of Thunder, Hear My Cry* sounds like a good book to read? Why or why not? Write what you think on the lines below.

_____

_____

Think About the Story

Use Story Words

◆ **Directions:** Look at your list of story words on page 83. Write a story word on each line.

2. This book was _____ in 1976.

3. Cassie got _____ by the storekeeper.

4. A _____ practices law.

5. The Logans didn't have enough money for the land _____.

6. Another word for land is _____.

7. The scene where Cassie goes to town is _____.

8. People often _____ books to one another.

How Did They Feel?

◆ 9. How do you think Cassie and her brothers felt as they watched the bus break down in the ditch? Write about what you think on the lines below.

_____

_____

10. How do you think Papa and Mama felt when Papa was unable to go back to work? Write about what you think on the lines below.

_____

_____

Write Sentences About the Story

◆ **Directions:** Use words from the story to answer these questions.

11. Why is Cassie's family unusual?

_____

_____

12. Why is the first day of school in October?

_____

_____

13. Why is Cassie scolded by the storekeeper?

_____

_____

Words and Meanings

◆ **Directions:** Think about how the **bold** words are used in the story. Then circle the words that show the meaning of each word or phrase.

14. Money is so **scarce** that they have a hard time making the payment on the land. What does this mean?
    a. They are scared.
    b. There is plenty.
    c. There's not much.

15. The Logans **iron out a deal** with a lawyer. What did this mean?
    a. They ironed clothes.
    b. They worked out a way to shop somewhere else.
    c. They sold him their property.

16. Cassie's Papa tells her that there are things to "**take a stand on.**" This means _____.
    a. Cassie should talk and act on her belief
    b. Cassie should stand up straight
    c. Cassie should always follow directions

17. The children watched the bus break down **with satisfaction.** What did this mean?
    a. They were upset.
    b. They were pleased at what happened.
    c. They felt sorry for the kids who had to get muddy.

Letters and Sounds

◆ **Directions:** These words all have the letters **ough.** Circle the words with the short **u** sound. Underline the words with the long **o** sound.

   1. though   **2.** enough   **3.** tough

> **TIP:** The letters **ough** can have different sounds. For example, the word **rough** makes the short **u** sound and the word **bough** makes the **ow** sound.

◆ **Directions:** Write each word in the box where it belongs.

sought	enough	through
cough	tough	though
trough	bought	rough

aw	long *u*	short *u*	long *o*
4. _____	8. _____	9. _____	12. _____
5. _____		10. _____	
6. _____		11. _____	
7. _____			

◆ **Directions:** Write the letters on the lines. How many words can you make?

th	t	s	f	b	en	thr

13. _____ ough   **18.** _____ ought

14. _____ ough   **19.** _____ ought

15. _____ ough   **20.** _____ ought

16. _____ ough   **21.** _____ ought

17. _____ ough

Story Words

◆ **Directions:** Read each word to yourself. Then say the word out loud. Write the word on the line. Check the box after each step.

22. gravity (grav│i│ty) Read ❑ Say ❑ Write ❑ _____

23. force Read ❑ Say ❑ Write ❑ _____

24. microgravity Read ❑ Say ❑ Write ❑ _____
    (mi│cro│grav│i│ty)

25. mission (mis│sion) Read ❑ Say ❑ Write ❑ _____

26. shuttle (shut│tle) Read ❑ Say ❑ Write ❑ _____

27. experiment Read ❑ Say ❑ Write ❑ _____
    (ex│per│i│ment)

28. advances Read ❑ Say ❑ Write ❑ _____
    (ad│van│ces)

Word Bank

Write each of these story words in the Word Bank at the back of this book.

More Word Work

You can add suffixes to words to change their meanings.
The letters **ly, ful, less,** and **ness** are suffixes.

Examples: The children walked slowly across the street.
Tom said the movie was wonderful.

◆ **Directions:** Add the suffix to each word. Write the new word on the line.

29. eager + ness _____

30. thought + ful _____

31. help + less _____

32. happy + ly _____

▶ **TIP:** When adding a suffix to a word ending in **y,** change the **y** to an **i.** For example, the word **clumsy** changes to **clumsily.**

◆ **Directions:** Read the words you changed. Write a word on each line to complete the sentences.

33. Newborn babies are _____.

34. When Jim helps his neighbor, he is being _____.

35. The children _____ licked ice cream cones.

36. Miguel shows _____ by raising his hand in class.

Use What You Know

Research in science is being conducted every day. What experiments or research have you heard of before? Maybe you have seen something on television, heard a report on the radio, or done an experiment of your own in school. Write about your experience on the lines below.

_____

_____

_____

_____

OUT OF THIS WORLD RESEARCH, PART 1

One hundred years ago, no one expected we would one day use our fingers to dial a number and make a telephone call. No one imagined really flying halfway around the world in a matter of hours. No one dared believe that medicine would truly bring an end to many deadly diseases. Research has made these things possible, and today people are used to them. New ideas in science have continued to allow us more discoveries.

When you think of scientific research, do you picture rows of scientists in white lab-coats, working in a university laboratory building? What you may find surprising is how much scientific research is now done in space. Today, a lot of work in the fields of biology, chemistry, physics, ecology, and medicine takes place beyond Earth's atmosphere.

You might wonder why research is being done in outer space. The reason is that there is no gravity in space. Gravity is the natural force that keeps us from floating off the earth. Gravity constantly pulls us toward the center of the earth. Because of gravity, we can toss a ball through the air and catch it as it falls back. Gravity makes snow fall to the ground. Gravity also hides things from us. Scientists sometimes want to learn how things grow and work when gravity is not around. When their research is free from gravity, the answers are often different.

The word microgravity is used to describe gravity in space. There, it is one millionth of the gravity here on Earth. A lot of microgravity research has taken place on space shuttle missions. The research takes place in the "Spacelab." The Spacelab itself is very small and has equipment stacked from floor to ceiling. The crew doesn't climb a ladder to enter. They float in through a tunnel.

Each mission, or trip to space, costs millions of dollars and takes many years of planning. Scientists must first present their research ideas to NASA, which stands for the National Aeronautics and Space

Administration. The ideas that are chosen must increase knowledge and benefit life on Earth. The first microgravity Spacelab was launched in January 1992 on the space shuttle Discovery. Discovery carried mice, frogs, crystals, wheat seeds, and hamsters in addition to all sorts of equipment. The journey was **all in the interest** of science.

One of the crew members on that mission was a scientist from Canada, Roberta Bondar. Some of Bondar's research was made in the biorack, an area of the lab made just for biology experiments. It was about the size of a small coat closet. As Bondar worked, she talked with scientists back on Earth, but no one ever shouted. They used special communication headsets. One of the experiments was to see how plants react to microgravity. On Earth, plants grow toward the light. Their roots grow downward. Scientists asked whether the roots would also grow downward in space. They wanted to know if a plant can find light in a weightless environment and how it decides which way is down in space. The data helped scientists find answers to these questions.

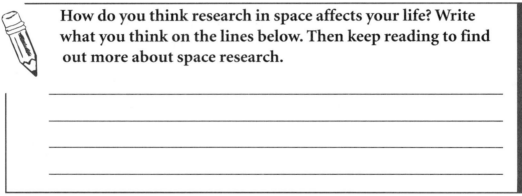

How do you think research in space affects your life? Write what you think on the lines below. Then keep reading to find out more about space research.

_____

_____

_____

_____

Other experiments helped the crew learn more about how the body reacts in space. On Earth, our bodies rely on the inner ear for balance. In space, the inner ear sends different messages to the nervous system. One crewmember spent time sliding while strapped to a sled. This test was to find out how long the inner ear and brain need to change the signals they send to the body.

How does all this research affect your life? **To date,** many advances and products have made their way back to Earth. One product is the special foam used in football pads, ski boots, and hospital bed pads. A stick control used by disabled drivers was invented for use in space. Another product is liquid-cooled clothing used for cancer treatment and spinal cord injuries.

Advances in science will continue on the new International Space Station (ISS). Many countries have worked together to build the ISS. The United States, Canada, Brazil, Japan, Russia, and 15 nations of the European Space Agency all used their knowledge, technology, and money on the project.

The ISS is more than four times the size of the Russian Mir space station. When the ISS is complete, it will have a mass of over one million pounds. It will be 356 feet across and 290 feet long. It isn't possible to run telephone poles or power lines up to the space station. For power, there will be many solar panels. These rectangle-shaped panels collect sunlight. They turn the heat energy into electrical power. The power will then be used by the space station. The power will also be helpful to scientists in their research.

In Part 2 you will learn about the new science lab of the ISS. You will also learn about research being done on the large, space-orbiting rocks we call asteroids. ▶

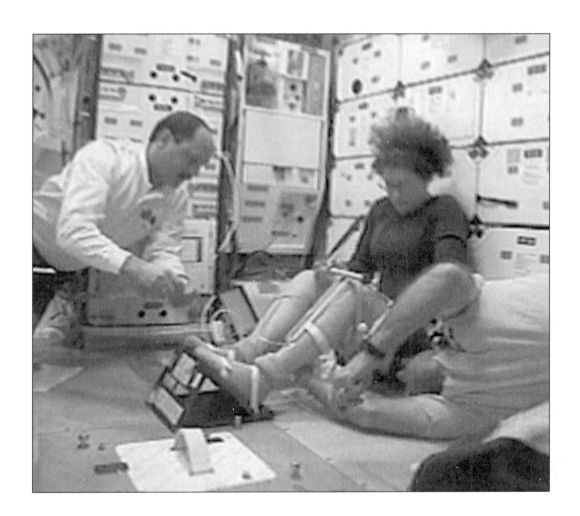

You Be the Judge

◆ 1. Do you think research in space is useful? Why or why not? Write what you think on the lines below.

_____

_____

2. What was the most interesting thing you learned from this piece? How come? Write about it on the lines below.

_____

_____

Think About the Story

Use Story Words

◆ **Directions:** Look at your list of story words on page 90. Write a story word on each line.

3. A scientist does not know how an _____ will turn out.

4. A space shuttle _____ is one trip.

5. Gravity is a _____.

6. To keep you from floating, _____ pulls at you.

7. Spacelab is a _____ lab.

8. Many _____ have been made from space research.

9. Discovery is the name of a space _____.

Write Sentences About the Story

◆ **Directions:** Use words from the story to answer these questions.

10. Why is some research done in outer space?

_____

_____

11. How are ideas chosen for space research?

_____

_____

12. How will the International Space Station get its power?

_____

_____

What Are the Facts?

◆ **Directions:** Write **T** next to the sentences that say true things about the story. Write **F** next to the sentences that do not.

13. _____ Hamsters have been in space.

14. _____ The force of gravity is greater in space.

15. _____ All scientific research is done on space shuttles.

16. _____ Foam used in football pads was developed in space.

Words and Meanings

◆ **Directions:** Think about how the **bold** words are used in the story. Then circle the words that show the meaning of each word or phrase.

17. Many living things were launched into space **all in the interest of** science. This phrase means _____.
    a. they will be used to learn more
    b. people are interested in science
    c. to make a TV show

18. **To date** many advances and products from space are being used on Earth. These words mean _____.
    a. in the future
    b. until now
    c. it never happened

Look Ahead

◆ 19. In Part 2 you will read about the lab on the ISS and research on asteroids. What do you think you will learn? Write two questions you would like to have answered.

_____

_____

_____

Letters and Sounds

◆ **Directions:** These words all have the **oi** sound, as in **coin**. Circle the letters in each word that make this sound.

   1. oyster   **2.** noise   **3.** boy   **4.** oil

◆ **Directions:** These words all have the **ou** sound as in **mouse**. Circle the letters in each word that make this sound.

   5. house   **6.** frown   **7.** town   **8.** mouth

> ▶ **TIP:** The letters **oy** and **oi** can each stand for the **oi** sound. The letters **ou** and **ow** can stand for the **ou** sound.

◆ **Directions:** Write each word under the words below that have the same sound pattern.

  out   soil   boil   clout   crown

  coil   soy   clown   toy   joy

foil	coy	brown	shout
9. _____	**12.** _____	**15.** _____	**17.** _____
10. _____	**13.** _____	**16.** _____	**18.** _____
11. _____	**14.** _____		

◆ **Directions:** Write the letters on the lines. How many words can you make?

c	s	b	r	w	h	br

19. _____ oil   **23.** _____ ound   **28.** _____ oy

20. _____ oil   **24.** _____ ound   **29.** _____ oy

21. _____ oil   **25.** _____ ound   **30.** _____ oy

22. _____ oil   **26.** _____ ound

                 27. _____ ound   **31.** _____ ow

                                        32. _____ ow

                                        33. _____ ow

                                        34. _____ ow

                                          35. _____ ow

                                          36. _____ ow

                                          37. _____ ow

Story Words

◆ **Directions:** Read each word to yourself. Then say the word out loud. Write the word on the line. Check the box after each step.

38. long-term   Read ❑ Say ❑ Write ❑ _____

39. astronaut   Read ❑ Say ❑ Write ❑ _____
    (as│tro│naut)

40. climate (cli│mate) Read ❑ Say ❑ Write ❑ _____

41. atmosphere   Read ❑ Say ❑ Write ❑ _____
    (at│mo│sphere)

42. orbit (or│bit)   Read ❑ Say ❑ Write ❑ _____

43. signal (sig│nal)   Read ❑ Say ❑ Write ❑ _____

More Word Work

You can add prefixes to words and change their meanings. The letters **de** and **non** are prefixes.

Examples: The number of snowboards sold this year decreased.
Younger people tend to be more nonconformist in their beliefs.

◆ **Directions:** Add the prefix to each word. Write the new word on the line.

44. non + sense   _____

45. de + frost   _____

46. non + smoker   _____

47. de + part   _____

TIP: When pronouncing a word using a prefix, the noun is accented on the first syllable.

◆ **Directions:** Choose two words that you made. Write each in a sentence on the lines below.

48. _____

    _____

49. _____

    _____

Use What You Know

Part 2 of this story tells about more areas of scientific research in space. One area focuses on asteroids. What do you know about these space rocks? Write what you know on the lines below.

_____

_____

_____

_____

OUT OF THIS WORLD RESEARCH, PART 2

In November of 1998, a space lab was shipped to the Kennedy Space Center in Orlando, Florida. The lab, named Destiny, took three years to build before its launch into space. Destiny is designed for long-term experiments that will be carried out over many more years.

The lab is quite small. It is 8.5 meters (28 feet) long and 4.3 meters (14 feet) in diameter. It has the shape of a cylinder, like a can of soda. The lab is even made of aluminum, which is the same metal used to make soda cans. The outside has a **waffle pattern,** which makes it strong. The outside is also covered with the same material used to make bullet-proof vests. This material protects the lab from objects flying through space, such as meteors.

In February of 2001, after Destiny was loaded into the bay of the space shuttle Atlantis, it was launched. Once it reached the ISS (International Space Station) Destiny had to be removed from the bay by a giant mechanical arm.

Marsha Ivins is the astronaut who controlled the arm on the Destiny. Like Destiny itself, Ivins also spent many years preparing for space. She knew that it would take a long time to reach her goal of becoming an astronaut. She started planning her career when she was ten years old. Ivins looked around and saw that all the astronauts were men. They were also military test pilots. She knew that being a test pilot wasn't possible, but she didn't give up. Instead she studied and worked hard to earn an engineering degree. Then she **landed a job** at NASA in the 1970s and she worked there for ten years. During that time, Ivins applied to the space shuttle astronaut program three times before she was accepted.

Once it was removed from the back of the space shuttle, whose giant doors **look like jaws,** Destiny had to be attached to the ISS. It took three space walks to do the job. A space walk is when an astronaut works outside the shuttle in open space wearing a special suit.

Do you think your life is affected by astronauts traveling in space? Circle your answer.

YES   NO

Then keep reading to find out more about space research.

Once in full operation, the ISS will enable scientists to view Earth as never before. ISS will be like a window through which we'll be able to see 75 percent of Earth's surface. From the rocky coast of England to the African plains, the world will be visible. This view will help scientists to better predict the climate over time and to see how the atmosphere is changing. Understanding climate will help farmers, fishermen, and the people who plan cities, since climate affects everyone.

This window on the world will also helps scientists study the environment. These studies will increase knowledge of our impact on the forests, oceans, mountains, and coastal areas. For example, in many countries people are cutting and burning forests to clear the land. Scientists will be better able to see the effects on the atmosphere. Air pollution, water pollution, and oil spills will all be studied. Scientists are also interested in looking at the effects on Earth's surface of volcanoes and old meteorite impacts.

Destiny will be used for many types of experiments and research in microgravity. In space, living cells can be tested for cancer treatments. New drugs will be developed without putting patients at risk. More powerful computer chips can be made because metals are more easily tested in space.

Do you think you would like to work in outer space? Why or why not? Write what you think on the lines below.

_____

_____

_____

_____

Not all research in space is done by humans. A recent study of the asteroid Eros was done by an unmanned spacecraft. The spacecraft was called NEAR-Shoemaker. NEAR stands for Near Earth Asteroid Rendezvous. It was also given the name Shoemaker, in honor of the late Eugene Shoemaker. He was an expert in Earth-crossing asteroids and impact craters. NEAR-Shoemaker spent most of the year 2000 in orbit around Eros.

Why is studying asteroids important? If the dinosaurs were still here, they would be able to tell you why. Many asteroids have struck Earth and the moon. Some people believe that 65 million years ago an asteroid or comet about 6 miles in diameter hit Earth. This led to the end of the dinosaur age. More recently, in 1989, an asteroid came within 640,000 kilometers (400,000 miles) of Earth. This may not sound very close, but in space it is considered a close call.

NEAR-Shoemaker was used to learn about Eros. The data collected provided clues to help figure out the asteroid's past, how the asteroid formed, and what it is made of. It turned out that Eros has more aluminum, gold, silver, and zinc than has ever been mined on Earth. This asteroid is worth more than several billion dollars in today's market for metals. The question is how to get these metals back to Earth.

After a year in orbit, NEAR-Shoemaker made history by landing on the asteroid. The scientists hadn't planned this, but thought it was worth the risk to get close-up photographs. The scientists sat with their eyes and ears open wide as NEAR-Shoemaker made its crash landing. At first, they didn't know if the landing was successful. This is because it takes 17.5 minutes for a radio wave signal to travel the 196 million miles back to Earth.

From Earth to the far reaches of space, the affects of scientific research are nonstop. There is one thing scientists are certain of: the universe has many secrets to unfold. They also realize that with new knowledge come many new questions to answer.

You Be the Judge

◆ 1. Do you think many people will someday live in space? Why or why not? Write what you think on the lines below.

_____

_____

Think About the Story

Use Story Words

◆ **Directions:** Look at your list of story words on page 97. Write a story word on each line.

2. Scientists will study the _____ using the ISS.

3. A _____ study happens over a long period of time.

4. NEAR-Shoemaker sends data with _____.

5. Pollution affects Earth's _____.

6. The ISS _____ or circles the Earth.

7. Marsha Ivins applied three times to become an
_____.

When Did It Happen?

◆ 8. Write a number from 1 to 4 in front of each event to show when it happened.

_____ The spacecraft orbited Eros and sent pictures and data.

_____ NEAR-Shoemaker was launched.

_____ The spacecraft made a crash landing on Eros.

_____ NEAR-Shoemaker traveled for 4 years.

What Were the Facts?

9. Circle the statements that are true about the ISS.

   a. The lab is named Destiny.

   b. It has 100 acres of solar panels.

   c. Scientists will study Earth's atmosphere.

   d. Research will be done to develop medicine.

   e. Every country in the world is helping to build the space station.

Words and Meanings

Directions: Think about how the **bold** words are used in the story. Then circle the words that show the meaning of each word or phrase.

10. Marsha Ivins **landed a job** at NASA. This means that _____.
    a. she helped land the space shuttle
    b. she decided to work somewhere else
    c. she got a job offer and began to work for NASA

11. The outside of Destiny has a **waffle pattern.** What does this mean?
    a. The metal has criss-crosses that look like a waffle.
    b. Scientists will study how to make the best waffles.
    c. Astronauts use waffle irons in space.

12. The space shuttle's giant bay doors **look like jaws.** This means that _____.
    a. there are teeth painted on the doors
    b. they transported sharks to space
    c. the doors open and shut like a large mouth

Write Sentences About the Story

Directions: Use words from the story to answer these questions.

13. How did Marsha Ivins prepare to be a shuttle astronaut?

    _____

    _____

    _____

14. What will scientists study from the ISS "window"?

    _____

    _____

    _____

15. What is special about the photographs from NEAR-Shoemaker?

    _____

    _____

    _____

Letters and Sounds

◆ **Directions:** These words have the short **oo** sound. Circle the letters that stand for the short **oo** sound in each word.

1. would 　　 2. wood 　　 3. should 　　 4. book

▶ **TIP:** The letters **oo** and **ou** can stand for the short **oo** sound.

◆ **Directions:** Read these words. Circle each one that has the short **oo** sound.

5. sew	8. hook	11. took	14. should
6. look	9. foam	12. wool	15. paste
7. could	10. geese	13. close	16. dishes

◆ **Directions:** Write each word you circled under the word below that has the same pattern of letters for short **oo**.

book	would
17. _____	21. _____
18. _____	22. _____
19. _____	
20. _____	

◆ **Directions:** Write the letters on the lines. See how many words you can make.

| b | sh | h | t | w | cr | c |

23. _____ ould 　　　　 26. _____ ook

24. _____ ould 　　　　 27. _____ ook

25. _____ ould 　　　　 28. _____ ook

　　　　　　　　　　　　　 29. _____ ook

　　　　　　　　　　　　　 30. _____ ook

　　　　　　　　　　　　　 31. _____ ook

Story Words

Directions: Read each word to yourself. Then say the word out loud. Write the word on the line. Check the box after each step.

32. athletic   Read ❑ Say ❑ Write ❑ _____
    (ath | let | ic)

33. rule   Read ❑ Say ❑ Write ❑ _____

34. defeat (de | feat)   Read ❑ Say ❑ Write ❑ _____

35. arena (a | re | na)   Read ❑ Say ❑ Write ❑ _____

36. professional   Read ❑ Say ❑ Write ❑ _____
    (pro | fes | sion | al)

37. ability (a | bil | i | ty)   Read ❑ Say ❑ Write ❑ _____

Word Bank

Write each of these story words in the Word Bank at the back of this book.

More Word Work

Directions: Write the two words as a contraction.

Example: she will   she'll

38. did not   _____

39. it is   _____

40. they are   _____

41. he has   _____

42. we had   _____

43. we will   _____

Directions: Write two sentences, each using a contraction.

44. _____

   _____

45. _____

   _____

Use What You Know

Do you have a favorite professional basketball team? What do you like about it? Who are your favorite players? Write on the lines below.

_____

_____

_____

_____

SLAM DUNK

Over a century ago, the *New York Times* printed an article with the headline "Girls Play Basketball." In 1910 a person from the Athletic Union stated that watching women competing in sports wasn't worth the trouble. At that time, people were not used to seeing women participate in sports. Today, millions of people watch women that play basketball—and play hard.

How did women's basketball become what it is today? It started in 1892 by a teacher from Smith College, a women's college in Massachusetts. Senda Berenson wanted to show her students the game. She changed the rules a bit and got her students playing. While this was happening on the East Coast, women from the West were also getting **into the act.** In this same year the University of California and Miss Head's School had their first game.

The first set of rules for women's basketball was published on March 13, 1895. The rules grew and changed over the years. In 1903 the halftimes lasted 15 minutes instead of 20 minutes. Until 1918 the game was played with a closed basket. There was a chain at the bottom. When a basket was made, the ball was caught. By 1972 women were playing under the same rules as men. The standard five-player, full-court game with a 30-second shot clock was used.

It was also in 1972 that President Richard Nixon signed the critical Title IX (Title 9) Educational Amendment. This amendment stated that in all school and athletic programs funded by the government, everyone is allowed to participate or play. The key to this was that, by law, no one could be told they couldn't play based on whether they were male or female.

Women's college basketball began to **draw some attention.** On January 27, 1975, the first-ever regular season game was put on national television. In a heart-pounding game, Immaculate College defeated the University of Maryland. The next month the team defeated Queens College, 65–61, in front of 12,000 screaming fans. This was the first women's college game to be played in New York City's famous Madison Square Garden.

The United States showcased its female talent in the Olympic arena. During the 1984 Los Angeles Olympics, the United States' team won the first-ever gold medal awarded for women's basketball. This was a reward measured not in cents, but in pride. The United States women's teams continued to flex their muscles by going on to win medals in 1988 at Seoul, 1992 at Barcelona, and 1996 at Atlanta.

Beginning in the 1970s, many people tried to create a professional league for women. In 1978 the WBL, or Women's Professional Basketball League, was formed. It lasted three seasons, but couldn't keep going. In 1991, 1992, and 1996, other leagues were formed. None of them lasted, but 1996 brought a **groundbreaking** decision by the Board of the NBA (National Basketball Association). They approved the idea for the WNBA.

On October 30, 1996, the first teams of the Women's National Basketball Association were chosen. The Eastern Conference was started with the Charlotte Sting, Cleveland Rockers, Houston Comets, and New York Liberty. The Western Conference began with the Los Angeles Sparks, Phoenix Mercury, Sacramento Monarchs, and Utah Starzz. The first players to sign on were Sheryl Swoopes and Rebecca Lobo.

The decision was made to have the WBNA play during the summer. The sports calendar was less crowded during that period, which meant that the games could be shown live on television. In that first season, over 50 million people followed the WBNA.

Have you ever watched a WNBA Game? Circle your answer.

YES   NO

Then keep reading to find out about one of the WNBA's first players.

Rebecca Lobo is 6'4", weighs 185 pounds, and has brown hair. Lobo grew up in a close-knit family in Southwick, Massachusetts. As a child she played any game she could—stickball, volleyball, Wiffle ball, and soccer to name a few. Even then she showed determination and an ability to practice with focus.

Lobo became a basketball star when playing for the University of Connecticut. Her parents were both teachers and were always there to cheer her on at her UConn home games. Even when her mother was battling cancer, she attended her games. During this difficult time Lobo stated, "Petty things don't bother me as much as they used to." Through it all, she kept up her near perfect grades and continued to be the leader for the UConn Huskies.

Her fans loved her then, as they do now. During college she did her best to answer every single letter written to her. This was no easy task, since mail arrived in the athletic office by the sackful. Lobo had difficulty being tough enough out on the court. Her coach wanted her to be more aggressive and not feel bad about hogging the basket. Lobo averaged over 17 points a game. During the 1997–1998 season, fans watched her perform as part of the WNBA team, the New York Liberty. An injury in 1999 forced her to stop playing for awhile.

Both on and off the court, Lobo has made the most of her abilities. She cowrote a book with her mother called *The Home Team.* She has appeared on many popular TV shows. She earned a degree in political science and plans a career in broadcasting.

The WNBA and the players are trying to make a difference everywhere. They have formed a group called "WNBA Be Active." It is a program that gets kids aged 11–14 involved in activities. Lobo and many other players work at basketball camps to give time to young players one-on-one.

The game of basketball and the women who choose to play it have come a long way.

You Be the Judge

◆ 1. Do you think the WNBA will be successful? Why or why not? Write what you think on the lines below.

_____

_____

2. How have the view of women and sports changed over the years? Write what you think on the lines below.

_____

_____

Think About the Story

Use Story Words

◆ **Directions:** Look at your list of story words on page 104. Write a story word on each line.

3. The WNBA is a _____ basketball association.

4. Players have to follow the _____ on the court.

5. Rebecca Lobo has _____ both on and off the court.

6. If one team _____ another, they win.

7. Women's basketball plays in the Olympic _____.

8. Men, women, boys, and girls can all enjoy _____.

The Big Idea

◆ 9. Which sentence tells what the whole story is about? Write it on the lines.

 a. The WNBA is watched by millions of people.
 b. Rebecca Lobo is a great player and person.
 c. Women's basketball and the people who play it have accomplished a great deal.

_____

_____

Words and Meanings

◆ **Directions:** Think about how the **bold** words are used in the story. Then circle the words that show the meaning of each word or phrase.

10. In 1892 women from the West were also getting **into the act.** This means that _____.
    a. they watched basketball
    b. they played basketball, too
    c. they liked to dive into pools

11. In the 1970s, women's college basketball began to **draw some attention.** What did this mean?
    a. People were interested in it.
    b. Artists drew pictures of the players.
    c. People liked college baseball more.

12. The NBA Board made a **groundbreaking** decision. This means that _____.
    a. they broke ground on a new stadium
    b. they dug a hole
    c. the decision was a new and important one

Write Sentences About the Story

◆ **Directions:** Use words from the story to answer these questions.

13. What does the Title IX Educational Amendment mean for women's basketball?

    _____

    _____

14. What happened because the WNBA began its season in the summertime?

    _____

    _____

15. How has Rebecca Lobo made the most of her abilities?

    _____

    _____

    _____

Letters and Sounds

◆ **Directions:** These words have the long **oo** sound. Circle the letters that make the long **oo** sound.

1. flute   2. boot   3. through   4. you

> **TIP:** The letters **ue, oo, u, ou, ew,** and **ough** can all stand for the long **oo** sound.

◆ **Directions:** Read these words. Circle each one that has the long **oo** sound.

5. grew	8. parachute	11. shovel	14. crew
6. tight	9. clue	12. hoop	15. pile
7. screw	10. door	13. June	16. blue

◆ **Directions:** Write each word you circled under the word below that has the same pattern of letters for long **oo**.

threw	glue	troop	flute
17. _____	20. _____	22. _____	23. _____
18. _____	21. _____		24. _____
19. _____			

◆ **Directions:** Write the letters on the lines. See how many words you can make.

| bl | tr | cr | gr | d | b | sh |

25. _____ ue   28. _____ ew   32. _____ oot

26. _____ ue   29. _____ ew   33. _____ oot

27. _____ ue   30. _____ ew

31. _____ ew

Story Words

◆ **Directions:** Read each word to yourself. Then say the word out loud. Write the word on the line. Check the box after each step.

34. flatlands (flat | lands) Read ❑ Say ❑ Write ❑ _____

35. temperature   Read ❑ Say ❑ Write ❑ _____
     (tem | per | a | ture)

36. degrees (de | grees)   Read ❑ Say ❑ Write ❑ _____

37. cacti (cac | ti)   Read ❑ Say ❑ Write ❑ _____

38. saguaro (sa | gua | ro) Read ❑ Say ❑ Write ❑ _____

39. guards   Read ❑ Say ❑ Write ❑ _____

More Word Work

◆ **Directions:** Combine the words to make a compound word. Write the new word on the line.

Example: book + mark = bookmark

40. flat   + lands   =   _____

41. snow + storm =   _____

42. gold + fish   =   _____

43. rain   + fall   =   _____

44. sun   + shine =   _____

45. day   + light   =   _____

46. wind + blown =   _____

Use What You Know

You are going to read about a special desert. Although no two desert areas in the world are exactly alike, all deserts are the same in some ways. What makes a desert? Write what you think on the lines below.

_____

_____

_____

_____

AS FAR AS THE EYE CAN SEE

You feel the heat rising around you. Nearby, you see a tall cactus and hear the shake of a rattlesnake's tail. Before you, windblown sands stretch as far as the eye can see. There is hardly a cloud in the sky. Far overhead, a hawk glides by a single cloud through a bright blue sky. Behind you, mountain ranges seem to explode from the flatlands. You are in the Sonoran Desert.

The Sonoran Desert covers 120,000 square miles of northern Mexico and parts of southern Arizona and California. It is the hottest of all the North American deserts. Summer temperatures can climb above 120°F. The ground can heat up to 180°F. That's just 32 degrees **short of** boiling. If you go, you had better wear a hat and sunblock, and carry plenty of water to drink.

What makes this place a desert? You might be surprised to know that it is not the hot sands and cacti. What makes all deserts the same is their lack of rainfall. A true desert has less than ten inches of rainfall or snow in a year. That is why the Sonoran Desert and the Sahara are deserts. Even the South Pole is a desert, because it gets so little snow every year.

Every desert is different. Their landscapes are not all the same, and their seasons are different. Of even greater interest may be the different kinds of plants and animals found in each.

The Sonoran Desert is alive with a **fair amount of** plants and animals. There are flowering plants and trees. They have interesting names like palo verde, cottonwood, desert ironwood, and aspen. There are snakes, coyotes, scorpions, mountain lions, hummingbirds, owls, prairie dogs, and many others.

What do you think might be the most important thing a plant or animal needs to survive in the desert? Write your answer on the lines. Then keep reading to find out more about the Sonoran Desert.

_____

_____

_____

Every plant and animal has learned to survive in the desert. The temperature drops sharply at night and then heats up again during the day. That is why many animals only come out at night, when it is cool. In the mountains, animals go into hiding when winter comes. This is because for every 1,000 feet you climb, the temperature drops about three degrees. And for the same distance climbed, the annual rainfall increases about two inches. Sometimes it snows. At that time of year, if you know where to look under the snow, you might find a short-horned lizard or a blacktailed rattlesnake. They sleep until warmer weather comes.

Many of the desert plants grow very close to the ground. This helps protect them from the very hot sun and the very dry air. A bush called the desert broom has very thin stems and small leaves that look almost like pine needles. Small leaves help a desert plant because they lose less water. Some plants can turn their leaves from the sun.

Something that makes the Sonoran Desert special is the many kinds of cacti that grow there. Cacti are plants that live only in dry areas, but they know how to save water. Their thick skin and spines guard them like armor against thirsty animals. The prickly pear and buckhorn cactus are common cacti, and they grow in the Sonoran Desert. But a special cactus you won't find elsewhere is the giant saguaro (say it like sa-war-o).

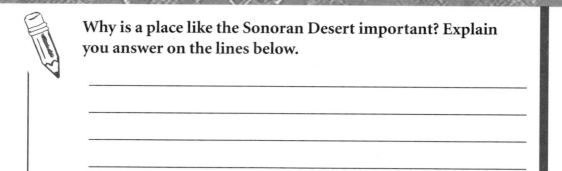

Why is a place like the Sonoran Desert important? Explain you answer on the lines below.

_____

_____

_____

_____

The giant saguaros stand like guards in the desert. They stick up tall and proud. The older saguaros have arms that grow out of their sides and point toward the sky. For many people they are symbols of the desert, symbols of survival. Some giant saguaros may be 200 years old. They can grow to a towering 50 feet. In just a few minutes they can send out many, long roots to gather water from a sudden rain storm. They can store a ton of water to survive for a year with no rainfall. Saguaros grow flowers and fruit, but like all cacti, they have no leaves. Two-inch spines help **ward off** hungry animals. There are many parts of the Sonoran desert that are thick with saguaros. You do not want to get lost in a cactus forest at night.

You might not want to experiment with the desert heat of the Sonoran summer. The fall or spring, however, are good times to plan a Sonoran Desert trip. The temperatures are not too bad, and as far as the eye can see, the sights are amazing.

You Be the Judge

◆ 1. Is the Sonoran Desert very different from where you live, or is it similar? On the lines below, write about how it compares to where you live.

_____

_____

2. Would you like to visit this North American desert? Why or why not? If so, what would you most like to see? Tell about this on the lines below.

_____

_____

Think About the Story

Use Story Words

◆ **Directions:** Look at your list of story words on page 111. Write a story word on each line.

3. The _____ cactus can grow to be 50 feet tall.

4. On a summer day the ground can be as hot as 180 _____.

5. Saguaros are like _____ in the Sonoran Desert.

6. The plural form of cactus is _____.

7. As you climb a mountain, the _____ drops.

8. Much of the Sonoran Desert stretches out into _____.

What Are the Facts?

◆ **Directions:** Write a **T** in the blank if the sentence is true. Write an **F** in the blank if the sentence is false.

9. _____ The Sonoran Desert is located at the South Pole.

10. _____ The Sonoran Desert has both flatlands and mountain ranges.

11. _____ Part of what makes the Sonoran Desert different is the types of cacti that grow there.

12. _____ The giant saguaro cactus is a flowering plant.

13. _____ The summers are very, very hot.

14. _____ Plants cannot grow in the desert heat.

Write Sentences About the Story

◆ **Directions:** Use words from the story to answer these questions.

15. What makes a place a desert?

_____

_____

16. Why are giant saguaros good symbols of survival?

_____

_____

Words and Meanings

◆ **Directions:** Think about how the **bold** words are used in the story. Then circle the words that show the meaning of each word or phrase.

17. The temperature of the earth in the summer is described as just 32 degrees **short of** boiling. What did this mean?
    a. It gets so hot that people will boil.
    b. The heat shrinks people.
    c. It's almost as hot as the boiling temperature.

18. Two-inch spines help saguaros **ward off** hungry animals. This means that _____.
    a. saguaros have a built-in defense system
    b. saguaros have thick leaves
    c. there are a lot of hungry animals in the desert

19. In the desert you can find a **fair amount of** plants and animals. What did this mean?
    a. There are few plants and animals.
    b. There are quite a few plants and animals.
    c. The plants and animals are not very interesting.

The Big Idea

◆ 20. Which statement tells the author's purpose in writing "As Far As the Eye Can See"? Circle the answer.
    a. to teach the reader what flatlands are
    b. to tell the reader about the beautiful and unusual Sonoran Desert
    c. to convince the reader never to go see the Sonoran Desert

Chapter 2 Summary of Skills and Strategies

Let's look back at what you learned in Chapter 2.

Letters and Sounds

◆ You learned that...

- the letters **ph** and **gh** can stand for the **f** sound in **cough.**
- the letter pattern vowel-consonant-consonant, or VCC, usually stands for a short vowel sound.
- many different letters can be silent.
- the letters **ough** can stand for different vowel sounds.
- the schwa sound **en** can be made by different letter combinations.
- the letters **oy** and **oi** can stand for the vowel sound in **boy.**
- the letters **ou** and **ow** can stand for the vowel sound in **town.**
- the long and short **oo** sounds are made by many different letter combinations.

Stories and Skills

◆ You learned about...

- characters who met challenges and solved problems.
- a famous book, *Roll of Thunder, Hear My Cry.*
- how scientific research is taking place in space.
- the history of women's professional basketball.

◆ You learned...

- how to use what you know to help you understand stories.
- how to look ahead, or predict, what story characters might do.

Words and Meanings

◆ You learned...

- to add the endings **ly, ful, less,** and **ness.**
- how to add beginnings to words to change their meaning.
- how to make and use contractions.

The chapter review will give you a chance to show what you have learned.

Part A

Summing It Up: Letters and Sounds

> ▸ The **f** sound can be made by the letters **ph** or **gh,** as in **tough.**
>
> ▸ Words like **tough** and **graph** have the vowel-consonant-consonant pattern, or VCC.

Directions: Write each word in the list where it belongs.

phase	pheasant	enough	cough
telephone	rough	phrase	trough

photo	tough
1. _____	5. _____
2. _____	6. _____
3. _____	7. _____
4. _____	8. _____

> ▸ The letters **w, g, k, b, h, t,** and **n** can all be silent.

Directions: Circle the words that have a silent letter. Write the letter that is silent on the line.

9. comb _____   13. listen _____   17. high _____

10. knee _____   14. swing _____   18. white _____

11. when _____   15. column _____   19. run _____

12. gnu _____   16. sand _____   20. knot _____

> ▸ The letters **ion** and **en** make the schwa sound **en.**
>
> ▸ Vowels that make the schwa sound are weak stress vowels.

◈ **Directions:** Write each word below under the word that makes the schwa sound **en** the same way.

lotion	silent	listen
talent	caution	ration

forgiven	station
21. _____	24. _____
22. _____	25. _____
23. _____	26. _____

▲
▲ ▶ The letters **ough** can stand for the short **u** sound as in the word **enough**, the **aw** sound as in the word **cough,** as well as the long **o** and **u** sounds.

◈ **Directions:** Write each word below in the list where it belongs.

sought	though	tough	enough
bought	through	cough	rough

long *o*	*aw*	long *u*	short *u*
27. _____	28. _____	31. _____	32. _____
	29. _____		33. _____
	30. _____		34. _____

▲
▲ ▶ The sound heard in **royal** can be spelled **oy** or **oi**.
▶ The sound heard in **brown** can be spelled **ow** or **ou**.

◈ **Directions:** Write each word below in the list where it belongs.

soy	noise	shout	boy
coin	found	house	crown
wow	boil	toy	frown

soil	joy	south	town
35. _____	38. _____	41. _____	44. _____
36. _____	39. _____	42. _____	45. _____
37. _____	40. _____	43. _____	46. _____

> ▸ The letters **oo** and **ou** can stand for the short **oo** sound, as in the word **book.**

> ▸ The letters **ue, oo, u, ew,** and **ough** can all stand for the long **oo** sound, as in the word **you.**

Directions: Circle the words with the short **oo** sound. Underline the words with the long **oo** sound.

47. would	**50.** hook	**53.** shook	**56.** grew
48. clue	**51.** blue	**54.** could	**57.** June
49. shoot	**52.** flute	**55.** hoop	**58.** wool

Part B

Summing It Up: More Word Work

> ▸ You can add the prefixes **de** and **non** to some words.

> ▸ The prefix **non** means "not."

Directions: Add **de** or **non** to each word below to finish the sentence.

1. part   Robert's plane will _____ at 10:00 A.M.

2. fiction   Most newspapers are _____.

3. profit   Churches are _____ organizations.

4. creased   The number of students _____ from 485 to 427.

> ▸ You can add endings to words to change their meanings.

> ▸ The ending **ful** means "full."

> ▸ The ending **less** means "without."

> ▸ The ending **ness** means "state of."

> ▸ The ending **ly** means "in a way that is."

◆ **Directions:** Add **ful, less, ness,** or **ly** to each word below to finish the sentence.

5. final Mom said, "Fletcher is _____ ready to go."

6. cheer A man who smiles seems _____.

7. breath Kyle was _____ after his six-mile run.

8. sad Some people show their _____ with tears.

▲
▲
▲

▶ You can use contractions to make two words read as one.
▶ An ' is used to show where the letters are removed.
▶ The words **will, not, is, are, has, had,** and **have** can all be used as contractions.

◆ **Directions:** Write the two words as a contraction on the line.

9. can not _____

10. you are _____

11. he will _____

12. she will _____

13. it is _____

14. we will _____

15. we are _____

16. he is _____

17. they are _____

18. would not _____

◆ **Directions:** Write two sentences that each use at least one of the contractions you made above.

19. _____

_____

_____

20. _____

_____

_____

Part C

Story Words

◆ **Directions:** Write the word from the list that matches each clue.

recommend   astronaut   defeat

saguaro   whirling   textbook

1. spinning round _____

2. a type of cactus _____

3. to triumph over another team _____

4. suggest something to somebody else _____

5. something that is read by a student _____

6. someone who travels in space _____

◆ **Directions:** On the lines below, write a word from the list to finish each sentence.

cacti   sternly   microgravity
scolded   continent   climb
rules   signal   temperature

7. To get the boys to listen, Robby spoke _____.

8. Experiments in space are done in _____.

9. The boys wanted to _____ the ladder.

10. Over the years, the _____ of women's basketball have changed.

11. The higher you climb a mountain, the cooler the _____.

12. _____ means more than one cactus.

13. You are hearing a _____ when you listen to the radio.

14. Cassie was _____ by a friend's parent.

15. The United States is on the _____ of North America.

◆ **Directions:** Read each word. On the lines below, write a number to tell how many syllables the word has.

16. orbit _____   19. professional _____

17. advances _____   20. degrees _____

18. force _____   21. thought _____

◆ **Directions:** Write the word from the list that matches each clue.

listen	**long-term**	**powerful**
double	**athletics**	**gravity**

22. over months and months _____

23. a force that pulls you down _____

24. twice as much as one _____

25. open your ears _____

26. having to do with sports _____

27. very, very strong _____

◆ **Directions:** Write a word from the list to finish each sentence.

climate	**guards**	**published**	**shuttle**
spiral	**twins**	**payment**	**flatlands**

28. Alex and Aidan are _____.

29. *Roll of Thunder, Hear My Cry* was first _____ in 1976.

30. The Sonoran Desert has many _____.

31. _____ is the type of weather an area has.

32. Robby went down the _____ slide with the boys.

33. The Logans were worried about making the land _____.

34. Saguaros look like _____ in the desert.

35. The space _____ delivers materials to the ISS.

Part D

Think About the Stories

Who Did What?

◆ **Directions:** This list has the names of people who were in the stories in Chapter 2. Write a name to answer each question.

Marsha Ivins   **Mr. Morrison**   **Roberta Bondar**   **Rebecca Lobo**
Robby   **Cassie**   **Alex and Aidan**

1. Who has to walk to school? _____

2. Who operated the arm on the space shuttle? _____

3. Who played for the New York Liberty team? _____

4. Who had to use a screwdriver to unlock a door?

   _____

5. Who did biology research in space? _____

6. Who went with Papa and Stacey on a shopping trip?

   _____

7. Who was found painting in their bedroom? _____

When Did It Happen?

◆ **Directions:** Write a number from 1 to 4 in front of each event to show when it happened.

8. _____ Rebecca Lobo injures her knee.

   _____ Rebecca Lobo tries out for UConn.

   _____ Rebecca Lobo signs with the New York Liberty.

   _____ Rebecca Lobo graduates from college.

9. _____ Alex, Aidan, and Robby go to the park.

   _____ Alex and Aidan get locked inside the bedroom.

   _____ Robby meets the twins.

   _____ Robby decides he likes his job.

CHAPTER 3

▶ **Lesson 1** . . . . *page 126*
"Learning Curve," Part 1

▶ **Lesson 2** . . . . *page 133*
"Learning Curve," Part 2

▶ **Lesson 3** . . . . *page 140*
"We're Not Alone"

▶ **Lesson 4** . . . . *page 147*
"Cicada Cycle"

▶ **Lesson 5** . . . . *page 154*
"A Talent to Lead"

▶ **Lesson 6** . . . . *page 161*
"A Man Ahead of His Time"

▶ **Lesson 7** . . . . *page 168*
"Teddy's Bear"

Letters and Sounds

◆ **Directions:** Many letters sound like the **aw** sound. Write the words on the lines. Circle the letters that make the **aw** sound.

1. taught _____
2. cough _____
3. call _____
4. Paul _____
5. awesome _____

◆ **Directions:** Circle the words that have the **aw** sound.

6. cloud　　**8.** crawl　　**10.** bowl　　**12.** join
7. mall　　**9.** autumn　**11.** recall

◆ **Directions:** You know the word **saw.** It has the **aw** sound. Many words end like **saw.** Write **saw** on the line.

13. _____

◆ **Directions:** Write these letters on the lines to form words that end with **aw.**

| dr | j | cl | r | l | str |

14. _____ aw　　　　**17.** _____ aw
15. _____ aw　　　　**18.** _____ aw
16. _____ aw　　　　**19.** _____ aw

◆ **Directions:** The words **bought** and **caught** contain the **aw** sound. Write **bought** on the line.

20. _____

◆ **Directions:** Write these letters on the lines to form words that end with **ought.**

| br | s | f | th | t | c |

21. _____ ought　　**25.** _____ aught
22. _____ ought　　**26.** _____ aught
23. _____ ought
24. _____ ought

Story Words

◆ **Directions:** Read each word to yourself. Then say the word out loud. Write the word on the line. Check the box after each step.

27. application   Read ❑ Say ❑ Write ❑ _____
(ap│pli│ca│tion)

28. schedule (sched│ule) Read ❑ Say ❑ Write ❑ _____

29. follow-up letter   Read ❑ Say ❑ Write ❑ _____
(fol│low│up│let│ter)

30. interview   Read ❑ Say ❑ Write ❑ _____
(in│ter│view)

31. concentrate   Read ❑ Say ❑ Write ❑ _____
(con│cen│trate)

More Word Work

◆ **Directions:** The ending **ion** means "the act or state of." Adding **ion** to a verb makes a noun.

Example: direct + ion = direction

Add **ion** to each word below.

32. correct _____

33. attract _____

34. complete _____

35. digest _____

36. communicate _____

37. evaporate _____

38. champ _____

39. act _____

40. confuse_____

> **TIP:** If the verb ends with final **e,** drop the **e** before adding **ion.**

Use What You Know

In this story, you'll meet Paul. He is waiting to hear if he has been hired for a new job. Work in a group. Make a list of the things Paul could do to improve his chances of getting the job. Then read on to find out what Paul does.

_____

_____

_____

_____

LEARNING CURVE, PART 1

Paul walked through the East Mall alone. He was going to buy some art supplies. On his way through the mall, he saw a sign in a store window. It said, "Now Hiring." Paul thought about it, then went in and talked to Mr. Lee, the storeowner. He told Mr. Lee that he wanted to apply for the job. Mr. Lee gave Paul a single sheet of paper. Paul carefully filled out the application. He checked it to make sure the information was correct.

Mr. Lee looked over the form. He asked Paul about his grades in school and his outside activities. "I have one more question for you," Mr. Lee said. "When would you be able to start work?"

Paul felt his **mouth go dry.** His schedule was very busy for the next week. He had to complete a drawing for an art contest. He had also promised to help his father do some work in the yard. Paul thought for a moment. "I have some things I must do this week, but I could begin next week."

"That's fine, Paul. I need some time to look over the other applications," Mr. Lee said. "I'll call you on Monday to let you know if you have the job."

On his way home, Paul thought a lot about the job. He knew that other people wanted it, too. He tried to think of something he could do to make his application **stand out from the others.**

Will Paul find a way to make his application stand out from the others so he lands the job? Circle your answer.

YES   NO

Then keep reading to find out what happens.

Paul called his friend, Carla. She had just been hired to work in another store at the mall. He asked Carla how she had gotten her job. "I sent the storeowner a follow-up letter," she told him.

"Why did you do that?" Paul asked.

"To express my thanks for the interview," explained Carla. "I said it was kind of the storeowner to take the time to see me. I also made sure he knew that I was very eager to work in his store. If you really want the job, then write a follow-up letter," she said.

"What should I include in the letter?" Paul asked.

"Start off by typing your address on the top right corner of the page. Then put the date below your address," Carla explained.

"Then do I type a greeting?" said Paul.

"No," Carla answered. "You type the address of the person you are writing to. Since you are writing to a storeowner, start with the name of the store. Then type the address. After that, you type the greeting."

"What do you think I should say in the body of the letter?" asked Paul.

"You should thank Mr. Lee for the interview. Tell him that you hope he will hire you. Let him know that you really want the job," suggested Carla.

Paul did just that. He typed a short follow-up letter, which is one kind of business letter. He made sure to follow all of Carla's directions. He had his Mom read it over to make sure it didn't have any mistakes. Then Paul mailed the letter.

How do you think a follow-up letter can help a person get a job? Write what you think on the lines below.

_____

_____

_____

_____

A week later, Paul was waiting for Mr. Lee's call. He tried to work on a drawing, but the artist seemed to have lost his **touch.** He wasn't getting much done. That's because Paul could not concentrate on his art. He was too busy thinking about Mr. Lee's promise.

"Why doesn't Mr. Lee call?" he thought. "He said he would let me know if I had the job today."

Suddenly, the phone rang. It was the call Paul had been waiting for.

"I have good news for you," Mr. Lee said. "I've decided to hire you for the job. That is, if you still want it."

"Of course I do," said Paul. "I've been thinking about it all week. I was starting to worry that you had decided to hire someone else."

"Well, I did have a number of people to choose from," Mr. Lee said. "But you were the only person who sent me a letter after the interview. That letter told me a lot about you, Paul. It showed me that you are serious about the job. That's the kind of person I want working for me," Mr. Lee explained.

"I am serious about the job," Paul said. "I'm also very thankful. You won't be sorry you hired me, Mr. Lee." ▶

You Be the Judge

◆ 1. If you were Mr. Lee, would you have hired Paul? Why or why not? Talk about this with a group of friends. Write what you think on the lines below.

_____

_____

Think About the Story

Use Story Words

◆ **Directions:** Look at your list of story words on page 127. Write a story word on each line.

2. Carla said that Paul should send Mr. Lee a _____ .

3. Mr. Lee asked Paul to fill out an _____ .

4. It was hard for Paul to _____ on his drawing.

5. Paul's _____ was busy for the next week.

6. Mr. Lee _____ Paul for the job.

Words and Meanings

◆ **Directions:** Think about how the **bold** words are used in the story. Then circle the words that show the meaning.

7. Paul felt his **mouth go dry** because he was _____.
   a. hungry
   b. nervous
   c. busy

8. Paul wanted his application **to stand out from the others** because he _____.
   a. couldn't start work right away
   b. didn't want to make Carla mad
   c. wanted Mr. Lee to notice him

9. In this story, **touch** means _____.
   a. able to do something
   b. to feel something
   c. to squeeze an item

Write Sentences About the Story

◆ **Directions:** Use words from the story to answer these questions.

10. Why did Paul feel that he needed to do more to get the job?

_____

_____

11. What do you write in a follow-up letter?

_____

_____

12. Why did Mr. Lee hire Paul?

_____

_____

When Did It Happen?

◆ 13. Write a number from 1 to 5 in front of each item to show when it happened.

_____ Paul called Carla.

_____ Mr. Lee told Paul he had the job.

_____ Paul filled out an application.

_____ Paul typed a follow-up letter.

_____ Paul saw a sign in the store window.

Your Turn

◆ 14. Suppose you were Paul. Write the first two sentences of a follow-up letter to Mr. Lee to let him know that you are eager to work in his store.

_____

_____

Look Ahead

◆ 15. What do you think Paul's first day on the job will be like? What kinds of things will Mr. Lee ask him to do? Write what you think will happen on the lines below.

_____

_____

_____

Letters and Sounds

◆ **Directions:** The word **store** ends with the **or** sound. Other letter combinations also make the **or** sound. Circle the letters that make the **or** sound.

1. store   2. oar   3. porch   4. pour

◆ **Directions:** Write these letters on the lines to form words that end with **ore**.

| ch | | r | | t | | c | | p | | b |

5. _____ ore   8. _____ ore

6. _____ ore   9. _____ ore

7. _____ ore

◆ **Directions:** Circle and write the letters that make the **or** sound.

10. door _____

11. roar _____

12. four _____

13. war _____

14. for _____

◆ **Directions:** Circle the words that have the **or** sound.

15. flood   17. soar   19. order   21. road

16. report   18. pour   20. cloud   22. yourself

Story Words

◆ **Directions:** Read each word to yourself. Then say the word out loud. Write the word on the line. Check the box after each step.

23. organized   Read ❑ Say ❑ Write ❑ _____
    (or | gan | ized)

24. reviewed (re | viewed) Read ❑ Say ❑ Write ❑ _____

25. immediately   Read ❑ Say ❑ Write ❑ _____
    (im | me | di | ate | ly)

26. tour   Read ❑ Say ❑ Write ❑ _____

27. government   Read ❑ Say ❑ Write ❑ _____
    (gov | ern | ment)

Word Bank

Write each of these story words in the Word Bank at the back of this book.

More Word Work

The prefixes **in** and **im** mean "not." Adding these prefixes to a word creates an antonym, or word with the opposite meaning.

◆ **Directions:** Add the prefix to each word below. Write the new word and its meaning on the lines.

Examples: ▸ im + polite   *impolite* means *using bad manners*

▸ in + ability   *inability* means *not able to do something*

28. im + possible _____ means _____

29. in + accurate _____ means _____

30. in + complete _____ means _____

31. im + pure _____ means _____

32. in + expensive _____ means _____

▶ **TIP:** Prefixes are small but important letters that are added to the beginning of a word, which then changes its meaning.

Use What You Know

In this story, you'll learn about Paul's first day on the job. Work in a group. Make a list of the things Paul could do to get ready for his first day of work. Then read to find out what Paul does.

_____

_____

_____

_____

LEARNING CURVE, PART 2

Paul had to report for work at 5 P.M. on Tuesday. He knew it was important to **get off to a good start.** He did not want to be late for his first day on the job.

Still, Paul had other things to do on Tuesday. First, he had to go to school. Next he had to go straight to baseball practice. After practice, he had to give his sister a ride home. Then he'd have to get to the store before 5 o'clock.

Paul knew he had to get organized. So he made a list of all the things he had to do on Tuesday. He also noted the least amount of time each task would take. Paul looked over the list. "Wow," he thought. "I have a very busy day waiting for me. I'll have to stick to these times. Otherwise, I'll never get to work on time!"

On Tuesday morning, Paul reviewed his list. As he went through his day, he checked off each finished item. Everything went smoothly until it was time to pick up his sister. She wasn't in front of the school as she said she would be. Immediately, Paul began to feel anger rise inside of him. "What's wrong with her?" he thought. "She knows I don't have a minute to spare!"

Just as he was ready to **lose control,** Paul's sister popped into sight. "Sorry," she said. "I had to go back to my locker for a book."

"That's okay," Paul answered, trying to keep his cool. "Just fasten your seat belt. We've got to get going!"

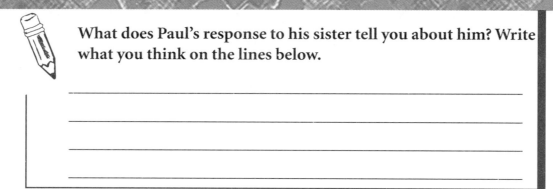

What does Paul's response to his sister tell you about him? Write what you think on the lines below.

_____

_____

_____

_____

At 4:50 P.M., Paul entered the store. Mr. Lee was waiting for him. "Welcome, Paul," the storeowner said. "Are you ready to learn how to run this place?"

"Most definitely," Paul responded. "What should I do first?"

Mr. Lee thought for a moment. "Let's start with a tour of the store. Then you will have some idea of where things are located."

For the next twenty minutes, Paul followed Mr. Lee around the store. He listened carefully to his boss. He asked questions and even took notes on a small pad.

When the tour was done, Mr. Lee gave Paul some papers. "I need you to fill out these forms," he said.

"What are they for?" Paul asked.

"The government," Mr. Lee said. "Every worker has to fill out tax forms. They determine how much of your paycheck is set aside for taxes."

Paul knew a little about taxes from math class. He remembered that all workers must pay taxes on their wages. He knew that part of his weekly paycheck would be taken out for taxes. Paul recalled his teacher explaining that every worker gets a **statement** at the end of the year. Paul's statement would report how much of his money had been put aside for taxes.

Paul read over the forms. He knew how to answer some of the questions, but he was unsure about a few items.

"Do I have to complete these now?" Paul asked his boss.

"It's up to you, Paul," Mr. Lee answered. "You can complete them yourself right now. Or, you can take them with you and have someone help you fill them out. I just need to have them back by the end of the week."

"I know these are important," Paul said. "I think I'll take them home with me. I'd like my dad to look them over. But I'll be sure to return them by Friday."

After work that evening, Paul sat down with his dad. Together they completed the forms. Then they both checked their work. Paul didn't want anything to be incorrect. He knew that even a decimal point in the wrong place could cause big problems. Finally, both Paul and his father were satisfied with their work. They were both glad that Paul had landed the job.

You Be the Judge

◆ 1. If you were Paul, who would you ask to help you fill out the forms? Explain why you chose this person.

_____

_____

Think About the Story

Use Story Words

◆ **Directions:** Look at your list of story words on page 134. Write a story word on each line.

2. Paul had to fill out a tax form for the _____.

3. Paul made a list to help get _____.

4. Mr. Lee gave Paul a _____ of the store.

5. Paul _____ his list.

6. Paul felt anger rise in him _____.

Words and Meanings

◆ **Directions:** Think about how the **bold** words are used in the story. Then circle the words that show the meaning of each word or phrase.

7. Paul was ready to **lose control** because _____.
   a. he had missed baseball practice
   b. he didn't know how to fill out tax forms
   c. his sister was keeping him waiting

8. At the end of the year, Paul will get a **statement** that tells him _____.
   a. how much tax he has paid
   b. how many people work for Mr. Lee
   c. ways he can become a better worker

9. In this story, **get off to a good start** means _____.
   a. starting work early
   b. beginning something the right way
   c. arriving late for work

Write Sentences About the Story

◆ **Directions:** Use words from the story to answer these questions.

10. What did Paul do to help him get organized?

   _____

   _____

11. How did Paul show Mr. Lee that he was interested in the tour of the store?

   _____

   _____

12. Why does the government need to have Paul fill out tax forms?

   _____

   _____

When Did It Happen?

◆ **13.** Write a number from 1 to 5 in front of each event to show when it happened.

   _____ Paul and his dad filled out the tax forms.

   _____ Mr. Lee gave Paul a tour of the store.

   _____ Paul picked up his sister.

   _____ Paul went to school.

   _____ Paul attended baseball practice.

Your Turn

◆ **14.** Make a list of all the things you have to do tomorrow. Then divide the items into two categories. Make one category for the things you have to do in the morning. Make the other category for things you want to do in the afternoon.

   _____   _____

   _____   _____

   _____   _____

   _____   _____

   _____   _____

Letters and Sounds

◆ **Directions:** The word **burn** has the **ur** sound. Select a consonant to make another word with the **ur** sound. Write the word on the line. Circle the letters that make the **ur** sound.

1. _____

◆ **Directions:** Write three words that have the **ur** sound at the end.

2. murm _____

3. sl _____

4. sulf _____

◆ **Directions:** Other letters sound like the **ur** sound. Write these words on the line. Circle the letters that sound like the **ur** sound.

5. term _____

6. first _____

7. heard _____

8. person _____

◆ **Directions:** Circle the words that have the **u** sound.

9. bird, earth, ear, fewer, circus

10. late, learn, certain, tube, turtle

◆ **Directions:** All of these words are divided by vowel and consonant patterns into syllables. Write each word on the line. Circle the last syllable in each word.

11. hurdle _____

12. purple _____

13. turtle _____

14. circle _____

15. gurgle _____

Story Words

◆ **Directions:** Read each word to yourself. Then say the word out loud. Write the word on the line. Check the box after each step.

16. gear   Read ❑ Say ❑ Write ❑ _____

17. postpone   Read ❑ Say ❑ Write ❑ _____
   (post │ pone)

18. piercing (pierc │ ing)   Read ❑ Say ❑ Write ❑ _____

19. inhuman   Read ❑ Say ❑ Write ❑ _____
   (in │ hu │ man)

Word Bank

Write each of these story words in the Word Bank at the back of this book.

More Word Work

Using prepositions and prepositional phrases can make sentences clearer and more descriptive.

◆ **Directions:** Complete these sentences by using prepositional phrases. Choose from these prepositions.

   over   under   around   in   through

20. Jake carried his little brother _____ the woods.

21. Keisha swam _____ the surf.

22. The bridge was built _____ the river.

23. The fish swam _____ the boat.

24. The plane circled _____ the airport.

TIP: Prepositional phrases usually begin with a preposition and end with a noun or pronoun.
Example: Wendy walked **under the bridge.**

Use What You Know

In this story, you learn about what can happen when you let your imagination get the better of you. Work in a group. Discuss times when you thought something was real only to discover that your imagination was playing tricks on you.

_____

_____

_____

_____

WE'RE NOT ALONE

Wendy threw a clean shirt into her backpack. "That's it," she said to herself. "I'm finally ready to go."

Suddenly, the telephone rang. Wendy quickly answered the phone. It was her best friend, Jen.

"I've got bad news," Jen began. "I'm not going to make the camping trip."

Wendy was disappointed. They had planned the trip for weeks. Three classmates from their first period class were coming, too.

"You're kidding, right?" Wendy said. "This trip was your idea. Remember?"

"I know," Jen said. "But when we made our plans, I figured I'd be feeling okay."

"What's wrong?" Wendy asked.

"I'm not sure," answered her friend. "Either I ate something that doesn't agree with me, or I've got the flu. My stomach is killing me. Anyway, there's no way I can go camping like this."

"I suppose we could postpone the trip," said Wendy.

"No way!" replied Jen. "Why should everyone be disappointed? You guys go ahead without me."

"Then I'd better **get a move on.** I have to pick up Carla in ten minutes. Take care of yourself, Jen. We'll miss you."

Wendy hung up the phone. She had to race to the bank before meeting Carla.

Do you think the others will have a good time camping without Jen? Circle your answer.

YES   NO

Then keep reading to find out what takes place.

Several hours later, Wendy, Carla, Dee, and Tia were unpacking their gear. They set up their tents where there was a small clearing in the thick woods. In the center of the campsite, the girls built a huge campfire. Flames shot upward, piercing the darkness of the night. Shadows caused by the glowing flames danced across the sides of the tents. The only sound that could be heard was the crackling of burning twigs.

The campers sat around the fire cooking marshmallows. "Gosh, these woods look scary at night," said Tia as she began to roast a marshmallow. "Do you think anything lives in them?"

Dee chuckled to herself. "Of course there are things living in these woods," she said to her friend. "And every one of them is a living, breathing creature. They have just as much right to be here as you and I do. In fact, we are the strangers, not them. We should leave their home exactly as we found it. Let's be sure to pick up the trash and check that the fire is completely out before we go to sleep."

"Dee's right," added Carla. "Do you realize how often animals are harmed by campers? A few weeks ago, a campfire that wasn't put out completely started a huge forest fire. I wouldn't even guess how many animals lost their homes in that fire."

Suddenly, the girls were interrupted by the sound of a **high-pitched shriek.** It sounded inhuman. They looked at each other nervously. "What in the world was that?" asked Tia.

"Sounded like a scream to me," said Wendy.

"Yes, a scream made by something that was in great pain," said Dee.

Tia turned to Dee. "You don't think any large animals live in these woods, do you?"

"Well, that all depends," answered Dee.

"Depends on what?" said Tia in a puzzled voice.

"Depends on whether you think a bear is a large animal," Dee explained. "I know for a fact that bears have been seen in these woods. My mother has a friend who saw a big bear while camping with her friend last month. She said the bear came right up to their tent."

"Did it attack them?" asked Wendy.

"No. It just wanted to share a bit of their food. First it **downed** an entire bag of sunflower seeds. Then the bear stole sandwiches right out of their cooler. The woman and her friend were scared to death, and ran for their car. They watched the bear select food and take it back into the woods with him. They said it was like watching a bear go shopping in a supermarket." The girls started laughing.

The loud crack of a breaking branch stopped their laughter. Two of the girls jumped to their feet.

"Okay, that's enough animal stories for me," said Carla. "I'm starting to get nervous."

"Sshh!" warned Tia. "Listen. I heard something. We are definitely not alone."

The campers listened carefully. Tia was right. More sounds were coming from the woods. It sounded like someone—or something—was dragging metal wire across stones.

"I'm getting really scared," said Wendy.

"The sounds are coming closer," said Tia. "Maybe we should get into the car."

Before anyone could respond, a dark figure burst from the woods.

"Hi, guys! I knew you weren't having any fun without me!" It was Jen!

"When I started feeling much better, I decided to follow you," said Jen. She was dragging an enormous pack behind her. "I guess you heard me when my shoulder strap broke."

"Yeah, you got that right," said Wendy. "In fact you have no idea how glad we are to see you! We'll fix your pack in the morning."

You Be the Judge

◆ 1. If you were on the camping trip, what would you have done upon hearing sounds coming from the woods? Write what you think on the lines below.

_____

_____

Think About the Story

Use Story Words

◆ **Directions:** Look at your list of story words on page 141. Write a story word on each line.

2. The campers had to unpack their _____.

3. Jen told Wendy not to _____ the trip.

4. The campers stopped talking when they heard a shriek that sounded _____.

5. The flames were _____ the darkness.

Write Sentences About the Story

◆ **Directions:** Use words from the story to answer these questions.

6. Why is Wendy disappointed?

_____

_____

7. How do Wendy and the other girls react when they hear sounds in the woods?

_____

_____

8. How does Wendy feel when Jen appears?

_____

_____

Words and Meanings

Directions: Think about how the **bold** words are used in the story. Then circle the words that show the meaning.

9. When Wendy says that she has to **"get a move on,"** she means that she _____.

   a. wants to visit Jen

   b. needs to leave

   c. enjoys talking to her friend

10. A **high-pitched shriek** is a _____.

    a. growl

    b. loud scream

    c. banging sound

11. **Downed** means _____.

    a. to eat quickly

    b. to throw something

    c. to step on something

When Did It Happen?

12. Write a number from 1 to 5 in front of each event to show when it happened.

    _____ Jen got sick.

    _____ Carla told the campers about a forest fire.

    _____ Jen came up with the idea to go camping.

    _____ Jen reached the campsite.

    _____ Wendy picked up Carla.

Letters and Sounds

◆ **Directions:** The word **party** has the **ar** sound. Write **party** on the line. Circle the letters that make the **ar** sound.

   1. _____

◆ **Directions:** Write these words on the lines. Circle the letters that stand for the **ar** sound.

   2. carpet _____

   3. large _____

   4. sharp _____

   5. hearth _____

   6. army _____

   7. heart _____

> **TIP:** The letters **ar** and **ear** can stand for the **ar** sound.

◆ **Directions:** Circle the words that have the **ar** sound.

   8. farmer   **9.** raised   **10.** bear   **11.** star

◆ **Directions:** Circle the words that have the **ar** sound.

   12. reaction   **14.** argument   **16.** prediction   **18.** impartial

   13. dishearten   **15.** wearable   **17.** artistic   **19.** carpenter

◆ **Directions:** Split the words below into three syllables.

   20. artistic _____   **23.** argument _____

   21. impartial _____   **24.** dishearten _____

   22. carpenter _____

Story Words

♦ **Directions:** Read each word to yourself. Then say the word out loud. Write the word on the line. Check the box after each step.

25. cicada (ci | ca | da)   Read ❑ Say ❑ Write ❑ _____

26. mate   Read ❑ Say ❑ Write ❑ _____

27. hatch   Read ❑ Say ❑ Write ❑ _____

28. instinct (in | stinct) Read ❑ Say ❑ Write ❑ _____

29. cycle (cy | cle)   Read ❑ Say ❑ Write ❑ _____

More Word Work

A suffix is a group of letters added to the end of a word. Most suffixes have a certain meaning. Two common suffixes are **ly** and **ment.** The suffix **ly** means "in a certain manner." **Quickly** means "in a quick manner." **Simply** means "in a simple manner."

The suffix **ment** means "the act of." **Statement** means "the act of stating." **Movement** means "the act of moving."

♦ **Directions:** Add a suffix to form a new word. Write the word on the line.

30. safe + ly   _____

31. slow + ly   _____

32. quick + ly   _____

33. nervous + ly   _____

34. excite + ment _____

35. pay + ment   _____

36. treat + ment   _____

> **Word Bank**
>
> Write each of these story words in the Word Bank at the back of this book.

Use What You Know

You are going to read about an unusual insect. The word "insect" may make you think of flies or bees that travel easily through the air. Do you know there are insects that never fly? Write some facts you know about insects.

_____

_____

_____

_____

CICADA CYCLE

Insects are the largest group of animals on Earth. So far, scientists have identified about 750,000 types of insects. The list keeps growing. Each year thousands of new insects are discovered. Some scientists believe that there may be a million or more insects to discover.

Insects come in different shapes and sizes. Although they live in many different places and eat different things, they are all alike in certain ways. All insects have a body made up of three parts. All insects have three pairs of legs and two pairs of wings. All insects have a tough shell-like covering on the outside of their bodies.

Most insects are alike in another way, too. They change in size and shape as they grow into adults. These changes occur in **stages.** Different kinds of insects go through different numbers of stages. For example, butterflies have four stages of growth and development. Dragonflies go through three different stages of life. Some of these stages last only a single day. Some may last for a year or more.

One insect, the cicada, spends 17 years in a single life-stage. Cicadas are found all over the world, in places with average climates. Cicadas are commonly found in the Eastern and Midwestern parts of the United States where the weather and living conditions are just right for the cicada. An adult cicada is an average-looking insect. It has a short, wide body, six short legs, and two pairs of wings. Most are between 1 and 2 inches (2.5 to 5 cm) long. How the cicada grows to become an adult is a long story.

Adult male cicadas spend the summer resting in treetops. They announce themselves by making part of their bodies move back and forth rapidly. This creates loud buzzing sounds. When a large group of male cicadas rests in the same tree, their buzzing is a noisy chorus.

The males make one type of buzzing sound when they are angry. This sound is usually heard when something disturbs their perch. Another sound is made when the males are ready to attract female cicadas. The females move up the tree to join the males. After mating, each female cuts slits in the tree's branches and trunk. She lays between 200 and 600 eggs in these slits. Within a month of mating, both the male and female cicadas die.

 What do you think happens to the eggs hidden in the tree's branches? Write what you think on the lines below.

_____

_____

About six weeks later, the eggs **hatch.** Tiny, wingless cicadas fall from the tree. Bit by bit, these young insects dig into the soil. They will spend this next stage of their life underground. Some types of cicada spend 13 years growing and developing beneath the earth. Others spend 17 years underground. This life-stage of the cicada is one of the longest of any insect.

Like all living things, the developing cicadas need food. Underground, the young cicadas feed on the juices of plant roots for the strength they need to grow and change shape. Feeding also gives them energy to move through the soil. The young keep warm during cold winter months by moving deeper into the ground. They cool off during the warm summer months by moving closer to the earth's surface.

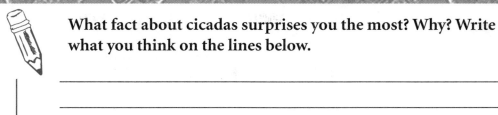

What fact about cicadas surprises you the most? Why? Write what you think on the lines below.

_____

_____

_____

_____

At the end of this 13- or 17-year stage, the cicadas are ready to enter their next life-stage. They move upward and pop out of the soil. Scientists do not know what **triggers** this action. Some scientists think that the insects feel changes in the soil. These changes may signal the cicada to climb upward and leave its underground home. Other scientists think that instinct causes the movement.

Back above ground, the adult cicadas begin their short final stage of life. After spending many long years buried alive, they have only a few weeks in the open air.

The cicadas, whose bodies have changed to adult form, slowly climb nearby trees. Sometimes, thousands of adults will move up the same tree trunk. As they move, the insects shed their hard skins. The thick outer coverings are caught in the plants and grass below. In some cases, an entire garden will be covered with cicada skins. Soon the males begin to sing their songs to attract the females. The adults mate and the cycle begins again.

♦

You Be the Judge

◆ 1. What do you think causes cicadas to leave their underground homes? Write what you think on the lines below.

_____

_____

Think About the Story

Use Story Words

◆ **Directions:** Look at your list of story words on page 148. Write a story word on each line.

2. The _____ insect is found all over the world.

3. Adult cicadas die about a month after they _____.

4. The life _____ begins when adult cicadas mate.

5. Cicadas _____ from eggs.

6. Some scientists think _____ causes Cicadas to move upward and out of the soil.

What's the Big Idea?

◆ 7. Which sentence tells the main idea of the selection? Circle the sentence.

    a. There are many different kinds of insects.

    b. The life cycle of a cicada is different from other insects.

    c. Cicadas are found all over the world.

Write Sentences About the Story

◆ **Directions:** Use words from the story to answer these questions.

8. What do the newly-born cicadas do after they hatch?

_____

_____

9. How long do cicadas live underground?

_____

_____

Words and Meanings

◈ **Directions:** Think about how the **bold** words are used in the story. Then circle the words that show the meaning.

10. Every insect goes through different **stages** means that _____.
    a. insects change shape
    b. insects live in different places
    c. insects have different periods of growth and development

11. When the cicada eggs **hatch,** they _____.
    a. break open
    b. roll to a new spot
    c. are eaten by birds

12. In this story, **triggers** means _____.
    a. parts of a weapon
    b. causes
    c. parts of an insect's body

Your Turn

13. Suppose you wanted to learn more about cicadas. Where could you get more information about these strange insects? Make a list of three places you would look.

    _____

    _____

    _____

Letters and Sounds

◆ **Directions:** The sound **ir** can be heard in many different ways. The letters **ir** in **irritate** make the same sound as the letters **eer** in **steer.** The sound in the letters **ear** in **beard** is the same as the sound in the letters **ier** in **fierce.** Read each word and circle the letters with the **ir** sound.

1. fear
2. sheer
3. irrational
4. irregular
5. clear
6. pier

◆ **Directions:** Write each word from the list above under the word below that has the same **ir** sound.

near	tier	irritate	deer
7. _____ 8. _____	9. _____	10. _____ 11. _____	12. _____

◆ **Directions:** Complete the words with letters that stand for the **ir** sound.

ir	ear	eer	ier	ere

13. h _____
14. h _____
15. app _____
16. sp _____

17. t _____
18. t _____
19. f _____
20. g _____

Story Words

◆ **Directions:** Read each word to yourself. Then say the word out loud. Write the word on the line. Check the box after each step.

Word Bank

Write each of these story words in the Word Bank at the back of this book.

21. senior (sen│ior) Read ❑ Say ❑ Write ❑ _____

22. auditorium Read ❑ Say ❑ Write ❑ _____
    (au│di│to│ri│um)

23. academic Read ❑ Say ❑ Write ❑ _____
    (ac│a│dem│ic)

24. requirements Read ❑ Say ❑ Write ❑ _____
    (re│quire│ments)

25. talents (tal│ents) Read ❑ Say ❑ Write ❑ _____

More Word Work

◆ **26.** When you need to come up with a good idea for writing, a cluster chart helps you to gather together words related to one central word or idea. Make groups of these words about baseball. Write them on the lines to complete the chart.

home run   strikeout   player   outfielder   coach

pitcher   walk   umpire   catcher

Ball	1. _____
Glove	2. _____
Bases	3. _____

BASEBALL

4. _____   7. _____

5. _____   8. _____

6. _____   9. _____

Use What You Know

A role model is a person that others admire and want to be like. A role model has many good traits. Some famous people are role models. Some ordinary people are role models, too. Think about your role model. Write a list of this person's traits on the lines below.

_____

_____

_____

_____

A TALENT TO LEAD

Mae joined the stream of seniors moving into the auditorium. The air was filled with the smells of new clothing and freshly waxed floors. Classmates who hadn't seen each other for nearly three months called greetings to one another.

Mae scanned the crowd for her friends. Hearing someone call her name, she turned toward the back of the hall. Her two best friends, Kim and Tia, were waving from the back row.

The ring of a bell indicated that the assembly was about to begin. Mae quickly squeezed into a seat next to her friends.

"Well, are you ready to begin your last year of high school?" asked Tia.

"Am I ever!" replied Mae. "I thought this day would never come."

Suddenly a sound like nails on a chalkboard screeched through the hall. Mrs. Dearborn, the school principal, adjusted the microphone.

"Welcome, seniors," she began. "I want to speak to you today about your last year of high school. I think I'll start by giving you the dates of special senior events."

The girls listened carefully as the principal noted the dates and locations of dances, assemblies, the senior prom, and graduation. Mae saw Kim marking the dates on a small calendar.

After discussing the month of June, Mrs. Dearborn moved on to a different topic. "Now, I need to tell you about a new program we're starting this year," she said. "You all know the academic requirements you must meet in order to graduate. This year, however, you also have a community service requirement to fulfill. Every senior is required to spend 20 hours doing some type of volunteer work in the community."

Everyone groaned loudly.

"I know what you are thinking," said the principal. "Where am I going to find twenty free hours? What can I possibly do to help the community? Well, twenty hours is about two hours per month. Many of you spend more time than that talking on the phone!"

"There are many places in our community that would welcome your help," she continued. "This morning you will receive a list of them. Before you read the list, take a minute to think about what you are good at doing. Think about your talents. Then look through the list for an opportunity to use your talents and serve your community."

Do you think Mae will find volunteer work that matches her talents? Circle your answer.

YES   NO

Then keep reading to find out what takes place.

At dinner that night, Mae told her mother about the new requirement. "What talents do I have?" she asked while digging into her salad.

"You have many talents," her mom replied. "You always enjoyed playing sports. I seem to **recall** you were once the best player on your soccer team."

"That was eight years ago in grade school," said Mae. "I was just a child. I'm a different person now."

"Well, you don't play soccer anymore," answered her mother. "But, you still know how to play the game. That talent will never desert you."

Mae thought about her mother's advice. She still knew how to play soccer.

"Maybe that's not such a bad idea after all," said Mae. "Let's take a look at the list."

Sure enough, the handout listed a youth group that needed someone to coach a girls' soccer team. The next day, Mae called the club director. Mae told the director that she would like to volunteer for the coaching job. Then she described her experiences playing soccer.

"You sound like a good person for the job," said the director. "The first practice is Saturday at noon. Why not come down to the field and I'll introduce the girls to their new coach?"

On Saturday, Mae walked nervously onto the field. "What am I doing here?" she asked herself. "I don't know enough about the game to be a coach. These girls will probably **laugh me right off the field.**"

The shrill sound of a whistle broke her thoughts. "Let's go girls," said the director. "Come meet your new coach."

A circle of ten-year-old girls surrounded Mae. They looked up at her as if she were a god. Curiosity and admiration gleamed from their faces.

Suddenly, Mae's mouth felt as if it was filled with cotton. She wondered if her players noticed how her hands were trembling. Gathering up all the courage she could find, Mae introduced herself. She told the girls that she had played soccer when she was their age. With each word, her nervousness decreased.

Feeling a bit calmer, Mae began to direct practice. Bit by bit, memories of her playing days popped into her head. She **drew upon** those experiences to help the players. Before she knew it, the two-hour practice was over.

When Mae returned home, she found her mother waiting for her. "Well, how did it go?" Mom asked. "Was it the longest two hours of your life?"

"Not at all," Mae replied. "The two hours went by quick as a wink. I think I actually taught the girls some new skills today."

"What about the coach?" asked her Mom. "Did she learn anything?"

"Yes," said Mae. "The coach learned that she has talents that can help others."

You Be the Judge

◆ 1. Why do you think the high school created a community service requirement for graduation? Write what you think on the lines below.

_____

_____

Think About the Story

Use Story Words

◆ **Directions:** Look at your list of story words on page 155. Write a story word on each line.

2. Every senior at Mae's school must fulfill graduation

_____.

3. Every _____ needed to spend 20 hours per week doing volunteer work.

4. One of Mae's _____ is knowing how to play soccer.

5. The students gathered in the _____.

6. Volunteer work is an _____ requirement.

Write Sentences About the Story

◆ **Directions:** Use words from the story to answer these questions.

7. What was the community service requirement for seniors?

_____

_____

8. How did the seniors know which community service work to pick?

_____

_____

9. What job did Mae volunteer for? Why?

_____

_____

When Did It Happen?

◆ 10. Write a number from 1 to 5 in front of each event to show when it happened.

_____ Kim jotted notes on her calendar.

_____ Mae spoke to the director of a youth group.

_____ Mae realized she does have special talents.

_____ Mae met her friends at the assembly.

_____ Mae introduced herself to the players.

Words and Meanings

◆ **Directions:** Think about how the **bold** words are used in the story. Then circle the words that show the meaning.

11. When Mae's mother **recalls** that Mae was once captain of her soccer team, she _____.

   a. finds her daughter's old soccer uniform

   b. remembers her daughter's place on the soccer team

   c. shows Mae pictures of her old soccer team

12. When Mae **drew upon** her experiences playing soccer, she _____.

   a. sketched them

   b. forgot them

   c. used them

13. In this story, **"laugh me right off the field"** means _____.

   a. being laughed at

   b. to carry away someone

   c. to fall

Your Turn

◆ 14. Suppose you wanted to act as a volunteer in your community. Write a list of talents you have that you might use for community service.

_____

_____

_____

_____

Letters and Sounds

◆ **Directions:** The letters **ear, air, ere,** and **are** can all stand for the **ar** sound. The word **bear** has the **ar** sound. Write the words below on the lines. Circle the letters that stand for the **ar** sound.

1. bear _____

2. chair _____

3. stare _____

4. there _____

5. pear _____

6. hair _____

7. carefully _____

◆ **Directions:** Circle the words that have the **ar** sound.

8. ready	**10.** garden	**12.** hare	**14.** pencil
9. spare	**11.** rarely	**13.** these	**15.** glare

◆ **Directions:** Write the letters on the lines. See how many words you can make.

b	st	p	m	th

16. _____ ear   18. _____ air   21. _____ are

17. _____ ear   19. _____ air   22. _____ are

                                                  23. _____ are

20. _____ ere   24. _____ are

Story Words

◆ Directions: Read each word to yourself. Then say the word out loud. Write the word on the line. Check the box after each step.

25. hardware   Read ❑ Say ❑ Write ❑ _____
    (hard|ware)

Word Bank

Write each of these story words in the Word Bank at the back of this book.

26. software (soft|ware) Read ❑ Say ❑ Write ❑ _____
27. installed (in|stalled) Read ❑ Say ❑ Write ❑ _____
28. clients (cli|ents)   Read ❑ Say ❑ Write ❑ _____
29. genius (gen|ius)   Read ❑ Say ❑ Write ❑ _____

More Word Work

A suffix is a group of letters added to the end of a word. The suffix **y** means "similar to." When you add the suffix **y** to a noun, you form an adjective. When you add the suffix **ment** to a verb, you form a noun. **Watery** means "similar to water." **Waxy** means "similar to wax." The verb **pay** means "to give money to someone." The noun **payment** means "what you give to someone, such as money, when you pay them."

◆ Directions: Add the suffix **y** or **ment** to form a new word. Write the word on the line.

30. rain + y   _____

31. sand + y   _____

32. agree + ment   _____

33. judge + ment   _____

> **TIP:** Sometimes you must drop the **e** before adding the suffix **ment**.

Use What You Know

It's hard to imagine the modern world without computers. In this selection, you will learn about a person who helped make computers part of everyday life. Computers are used in businesses, homes, schools, and restaurants. Think about the many ways computers are used. Write three sentences about how your life would be different without this important tool.

_____

_____

_____

_____

A MAN AHEAD OF HIS TIME

Fifty years ago, computers were found only in science labs and **military sites.** These early computers were so huge that they took up entire rooms. At that time they cost a great deal of money. In the 1950s, very few people knew how to use these tools.

Companies that made computers worked hard to improve their products. After a lot of effort, they learned how to make computers smaller and less expensive to own.

By the 1970s, the hardware that makes up the parts of a computer system was smaller and easier to put together. But the software used to operate the machines was difficult to use. Also, the commands that tell a computer how to work were too difficult for ordinary people to use.

A 20-year-old college student named Bill Gates changed computer operating systems. From the time he was a teenager, Gates was interested in computers. When he was 13, his school bought a computer. Gates immediately fell in love with the machine. He spent many hours working on it. Gates discovered a classmate named Paul Allen who shared his interest. The two teens became close friends. They spent all their free time on the computer. They even taught themselves to write a system of commands for the computer. One of their programs helped the school make student schedules. Gates and Allen were paid $4,200 for their program.

The two young men decided to use their knowledge of computers and go into business. In tenth grade, they formed a company. They used computers to study the traffic patterns of their hometown, Seattle, Washington. Other businesses paid for this information. In a short time, their company made over $20,000.

 What does this tell you about the information the company supplied to businesses? Write what you think on the lines below.

_____

_____

After graduation, Gates and Allen went their separate ways. Gates went to Harvard University. Allen went to work at a company near Harvard. One day, Allen paid a visit to his old friend. He brought a magazine story he wanted to show Gates. The story described a new type of computer that was smaller and faster than any other on the market. The two friends were amazed to read that the computer lacked an operating system to work. In order to work, the computer needed software, or a program of commands.

Gates and Allen already had a history of writing programs together. If they could develop an operating system for this new tool, they would get their big break.

The young men decided to make a **bold move.** They placed a call to New Mexico, where the computer company was located. After a few tries, they reached the company's president. To get his attention, they told him that they had created an operating system for his computer. The company president was interested in their program. He invited Gates and Allen to New Mexico for a demonstration.

Now Gates and Allen realized they were in a panic. They had only a few weeks to write the program. They started work immediately. Gates missed most of his classes. Allen took off many days from his job. The pair worked day and night. Their effort paid off. With the meeting just days away, they finished the program.

What do you think happens in New Mexico? Write what you think on the lines below.

_____

_____

_____

_____

The men decided that Allen would go to New Mexico to show their program. A very nervous Allen installed the program in the company's computer. It worked on the first try! The company's officials were impressed. They bought the system and hired Gates and Allen to write more programs.

Allen returned to Massachusetts with the good news. The men knew they couldn't continue to work and go to school while running a business. Gates left Harvard, and Allen left his job. The pair moved to New Mexico and formed a software company there. The company took on new clients and grew very quickly.

In 1979, the men moved their business to their hometown of Seattle. Soon after the move, another client contacted them. This client wanted Gates and Allen to write an operating system for its first personal computer. Gates reworked an old system and sold it to the client.

The client's personal computer was a **big hit.** Thousands of the computers were sold worldwide. Each one ran on Gates's operating system. The huge increase in their software company's sales made Gates and Allen rich men. Both were millionaires before they were 30. By the year 2000, Gates's fortune was more than $6 billion. The boy genius is now the richest man in the world.

You Be the Judge

◆ **1.** How did Bill Gates grow from being a millionaire at age 30 to a billionaire by age 40? Write your answer on the lines below.

_____

_____

Think About the Story

Use Story Words

◆ **Directions:** Look at your list of story words on page 162. Write a story word on each line.

2. Gates and Allen created _____ for their school's computer.

3. An operating system must be _____ in order for a computer to do work.

4. The men's company grew as it took on new _____.

5. _____ includes the parts of a computer.

6. Some people think Gates is a _____.

Why Did It Happen?

◆ **Directions:** Draw a line from each story event to the reason it happened.

What Happened	Why
7. Gates and Allen moved to New Mexico.	○ Gates couldn't run a business while going to school.
8. Gates dropped out of Harvard.	○ Every personal computer sold by a client used Gates's operating program.
9. Gates and Allen became rich.	○ Their first client was located in New Mexico.

Write Sentences About the Story

◆ **Directions:** Use words from the story to answer these questions.

10. What does a computer operating system do?

_____

_____

11. What did the new computer made in New Mexico lack?

_____

_____

Words and Meanings

◆ **Directions:** Think about how the words in **bold** are used in the story. Then circle the words that show the meaning.

12. To say that a client's personal computer was a **big hit,** means that _____.

    a. it made loud noises

    b. everybody wanted one

    c. it was very large and heavy

13. If Gates and Allen made a **bold move,** they were _____.

    a. daring

    b. dishonest

    c. intelligent

14. In this story, **military sites** means _____.

    a. different types of weapons

    b. places with pictures of people in uniform

    c. places where members of the armed forces work

Your Turn

◆ 15. Imagine that you are the computer company president's assistant. Gates and Allen call and want to speak with your boss. You tell them that he is not in the office. They say that they need to speak to him about their program for the company's new computer. On the lines below, write the message you will leave for your boss.

_____

_____

_____

Letters and Sounds

> **TIP:** Homophones sound the same but have different meanings. Homophones are also spelled differently. These words are homophones with **r**-controlled vowels.
>
> wear/ where   hair/ hare   there/their

◆ **Directions:** Read these words. They all have **r**-controlled vowels. They are all homophones. List all the homophone pairs on the lines below.

tear	herd	pore	horse
pour	stare	tier	here
stair	hoarse	or	
ore	hear	heard	

1. _____ _____

_____ _____

_____ _____

_____ _____

_____ _____

_____ _____

_____ _____

◆ **Directions:** Read these words and circle the letters that make the **el** sound.

2. travel   4. simple   6. usual   8. material

3. numeral   5. natural   7. table   9. possible

◆ **Directions:** Circle the homophone that completes each sentence.

10. Do you know (where / wear) Tim is?

11. He was (hear/here) this morning.

12. The players put (their / there / they're) bags on the team bus.

13. (Their / There / They're) playing for the state championship today.

14. (Their / There / They're) will be hundreds of fans at the game.

Story Words

Word Bank

Write each of these story words in the Word Bank at the back of this book.

Directions: Read each word to yourself. Then say the word out loud. Write the word on the line. Check the box after each step.

15. advantages   Read ❑ Say ❑ Write ❑   _____
(ad | van | tag | es)

16. abroad (a | broad)   Read ❑ Say ❑ Write ❑   _____

17. gymnasium   Read ❑ Say ❑ Write ❑   _____
(gym | na | si | um)

18. determination   Read ❑ Say ❑ Write ❑   _____
(de | ter | mi | na | tion)

19. politician   Read ❑ Say ❑ Write ❑   _____
(pol | i | ti | cian)

More Word Work

A suffix is a group of letters added to the end of a word. Most suffixes have a certain meaning. The suffixes **er** and **or** mean **a person or thing that does something.**

Examples: A **teacher** is a person who teaches.
A **sailor** is a person who sails.

Directions: Add a suffix to form a new word. Write the word on the line.

20. report + er = _____

21. invent + or = _____

22. travel + er = _____

23. farm + er = _____

Use What You Know

What do you know about Theodore Roosevelt? You probably know that he was called Teddy and that he was a president of the United States. Write the names of some other presidents on the lines below.

_____

_____

_____

_____

TEDDY'S BEAR

On October 27, 1858, a future president of the United States was born in New York City. At the time, no one thought Theodore Roosevelt would become a world leader. Teddy was a small child for his age. He was often sick and stayed indoors much of the time. He filled his days reading books. Teddy's poor health kept him from going to school like other children. He had to be taught at home by **tutors.**

Teddy grew up in a wealthy family. His grandfather was a well-known landowner and his father was a wealthy businessman. His uncle was a famous inventor.

Teddy had many advantages. Mr. Roosevelt often took his son on trips around the world. They spent months abroad, visiting Europe and the Middle East.

On days when he felt well, young Teddy explored the outdoors. He had a quick mind and was interested in nature. Plants and animals fascinated him. Even as a young boy, Roosevelt understood that humans share the earth with many other creatures. He never forgot this fact.

Once while visiting Maine, something happened that was to change Teddy's life. Two students who were traveling with him constantly teased Teddy. Because he was too frail to fight back, Teddy felt **ashamed** and helpless.

He later told his father what had happened. Mr. Roosevelt saw that his son needed to develop his body and had a gymnasium built in the family home. Teddy worked out daily. He grew strong and was sick less often.

Do you think that the things that happened to young Teddy will help him when he is older? Circle your answer.

YES   NO

Then keep reading to find out what takes place.

Roosevelt showed the same determination as an adult. He set goals for himself and worked hard to reach them. He graduated from college and decided to become a politician. Within a few years, he was elected governor of New York. In 1901, he was elected vice president of the United States. When President William McKinley died six months later, Roosevelt became president and led the country for the next eight years.

As president, Roosevelt helped change many things. He remembered his love for nature and created many new national parks. New laws preserved forests and saved the natural homes of many animals.

President Roosevelt also acted to protect people. He fought to control the power of big business. Laws were passed to make sure that workers received fair pay. Ordinary Americans felt they had a friend in the White House. They took an interest in everything the President did. Newspapers sent reporters on every trip that Roosevelt took because stories about the President sold newspapers.

One favorite story described what happened during a trip to Mississippi. Teddy decided to go hunting. Reporters and **aides** followed him for hours, but the President found nothing. Toward the end of the day, an aide found a lost bear cub. He tied the cub to a tree and ran to get the President. When Teddy saw the helpless cub, he set it loose. A reporter covering the event drew a cartoon showing the President and the cub. The reporter named the cub, "Teddy's Bear."

The cartoon appeared in many newspapers. A candy store owner in New York saw it. He asked his wife to make a stuffed animal that looked like the cub. They put the finished bear and the cartoon in their store window. The bear sold immediately.

The lady made two more bears and they sold, too. A steady flow of customers came to the shop seeking this new toy. Finally, the store owner sold his shop and started a toy company. He made thousands of Teddy Bears.

Both the toy and the President, who loved nature, remain popular today.

You Be the Judge

◆ 1. Why do you think teddy bears are popular with people of all ages? Write what you think on the lines below.

_____

_____

Think About the Story

Use Story Words

◆ **Directions:** Look at your list of story words on page 169. Write a story word on each line.

2. Mr. Roosevelt had a _____ built in his home.

3. The Roosevelts often traveled _____.

4. After graduating from college, Teddy decided to become a _____.

5. Teddy Roosevelt had many _____.

6. Roosevelt worked hard and showed much _____.

What's the Big Idea?

◆ 7. Which sentence tells what the selection is mostly about? Circle it.
   a. Teddy Roosevelt was small for his age.
   b. Teddy Roosevelt overcame many hardships.
   c. Teddy Roosevelt changed the way people work and play.

Write Sentences About the Story

◆ **Directions:** Use words from the story to answer these questions.

8. What was Roosevelt's response to being teased by two boys?

_____

_____

_____

9. What did Roosevelt do when he found the bear tied to a tree?

_____

_____

Words and Meanings

◆ **Directions:** Think about how the **bold** words are used in the story. Then circle the words that show the meaning.

10. To say that Teddy felt **ashamed** means that he was _____.
    a. unhealthy
    b. strong
    c. embarrassed

11. In this story, **aides** are _____.
    a. helpers
    b. friends
    c. businessmen

12. In this story, **tutors** means _____.
    a. teachers
    b. learners
    c. readers

Troublesome Words

Some words do not follow the typical rules, such as words with silent consonants.
Example: would

◆ **Directions:** Circle the silent consonants in the following words.

13. could   14. though   15. answer

Your Turn

◆ 16. Suppose you are an animal lover and want to write President Roosevelt about the young bear cub. Write a short friendly letter to show what you think about kindness to animals.

_____

_____

_____

_____

Chapter 3 Summary of Skills and Strategies

Let's look back at what you learned in Chapter 3.

Letters and Sounds

◆ You learned . . .

▸ the letters **aw, au, ough, augh,** and **all** can stand for the **aw** sound.

▸ the letters **or, ore, oar, our, oor,** and **ar** can stand for the **or** sound.

▸ the letters **er, ur, ir,** and **ear** can stand for the **ur** sound.

▸ the letters **ar, are,** and **ear** can stand for the **ar** sound.

▸ the letters **eer, ear, ier,** and **ere** can stand for the **ir** sound.

▸ the letters **air, are, ear,** and **er** can stand for the **ar** sound.

▸ that homophones are words that sound the same but have different spellings and meanings.

Stories and Skills

◆ You learned about. . .

▸ people who use their talents to find jobs and to start new businesses.

▸ a person who discovers a talent while doing community service.

▸ a president whose lifelong interest in nature benefits his country and gives one person an idea for a new business.

▸ an unusual insect that waits 17 years underground to become an adult.

◆ You learned. . .

▸ how to use what you know to help you understand stories.

▸ how to look ahead, or predict, what story characters might do.

Words and Meanings

◆ You learned. . .

▸ how to add suffixes such as **ion, ment, y, er,** and **or** to base words.

▸ when to use prefixes **in** and **im** to base words.

The chapter review will give you a chance to show what you have learned.

Part A

Summing It Up: Letters and Sounds

> ▸ The letters **aw, au, ough, augh,** and **all** can stand for the **aw** sound.

◆ **Directions:** Read each word. Circle the words that have the **aw** sound in **draw.**

1. laugh   3. bought   5. mall   7. beautiful   9. author

2. crawl   4. daughter   6. away   8. sought   10. taught

◆ **Directions:** Write each word you circled on the lines. Circle the letters that stand for the **aw** sound.

11. _____   15. _____

12. _____   16. _____

13. _____   17. _____

14. _____

> ▸ The letters **or, ore, oar, our, oor,** and **ar** stand for the **or** sound, as in **door.**

◆ **Directions:** Write each word on the lines. Circle the letters that stand for the **or** sound.

18. chore _____   21. roar _____

19. yourself _____   22. store _____

20. order _____   23. four _____

> ▸ The letters **er, ur, ir,** and **ear** can stand for the **ur** sound, as in **burn.**

◆ **Directions:** Write each word on the lines. Circle the letters that stand for the **ur** sound.

24. certain _____   27. first _____

25. term _____   28. learn _____

26. person _____   29. bird _____

▲
▲ ▶ The letters **ar, are,** and **ear** can stand for the **ar** sound, as in **garden.**

◆ **Directions:** Read each word. Circle the words that have the **ar** sound.

30. early   33. around   36. stare   39. dear

31. mark   34. large   37. party

32. carpet   35. heart   38. farmer

▲
▲ ▶ The letters **eer, ear, ier,** and **ere** can stand for the **ir** sound, as in **beard.**

◆ **Directions:** Write each word on the lines. Circle the letters that stand for the **ir** sound.

40. here _____   43. pier _____

41. fierce _____   44. appear _____

42. steer _____   45. dear _____

▲
▲ ▶ The letters **air, are,** and **ear** can stand for the **ar** sound, as in **stair.**

◆ **Directions:** Read each word. Circle the words that have the **ar** sound.

46. bear   49. carefully   52. stare   55. eat

47. paint   50. there   53. star

48. team   51. smart   54. chair

▲
▲ ▶ Homophones are words that sound the same but have different spellings and meanings.

◆ **Directions:** Read these words. Draw a line to match the words that are homophones.

56. wear   ○ fare

57. hair   ○ their

58. dear   ○ where

59. fair   ○ deer

60. there   ○ hare

Part B

Summing It Up: More Word Work

> ▸ A suffix is a word part that can be added to the end of a word.
> ▸ Adding a suffix changes the meaning of the word.
> ▸ The suffix **ion** means "the act or state of."
> ▸ The suffix **y** means "in a certain manner."
> ▸ The suffix **ment** means "the act of."
> ▸ The suffixes **er** and **or** mean "a person or thing that does something."

◆ **Directions:** Read these words. Circle each word that has a suffix.

1. rainy
2. order
3. direction
4. amusement
5. question
6. teacher
7. very
8. cement

◆ **Directions:** Write each word you circled on the lines. Then write the base word and suffix that make it up.

9. _____ _____ + _____
10. _____ _____ + _____
11. _____ _____ + _____
12. _____ _____ + _____

> ▸ A prefix is a word part that can be added to the beginning of some words.
> ▸ The prefixes **in** and **im** mean "not."

◆ **Directions:** Read these words. Circle each word that has a prefix.

13. incorrect
14. important
15. impolite
16. into
17. image
18. improper
19. indirect
20. inward

◆ **Directions:** Write each word you circled on the lines. Then write the base word and prefix that make it up.

21. _____ = _____ + _____
22. _____ = _____ + _____
23. _____ = _____ + _____
24. _____ = _____ + _____

Part C

Story Words

◆ **Directions:** On the lines below, write the word from the list that matches each clue.

application	immediately	organized	schedule
concentrate	interview	reviewed	tour

1. right away _____

2. a trip through a place _____

3. list of times when things must be done _____

4. form filled out by a person seeking a job _____

5. arranged a certain way _____

6. to direct one's thoughts on something _____

7. looked over or inspected _____

8. meeting between an employer and a person seeking a job

   _____

◆ **Directions:** On the lines below, write a word from the list to finish each sentence.

cicada	gear	piercing	cycle
hatch	inhuman	mate	postpone

9. The campers put their _____ in the van.

10. A _____ is an insect.

11. When do you expect those eggs to _____ ?

12. We will have to _____ the picnic due to rain.

13. Cicadas die soon after they _____.

14. Lightning bolts flashed, _____ the dark sky.

15. The life _____ of a human starts with birth.

16. Carla jumped at the sound of an _____ cry.

Directions: Read each word. On the lines below, write a number to tell how many syllables it has.

17. auditorium _____   19. requirements _____

18. academic _____   20. talents _____

Directions: On the lines below, write the word from the list that matches each clue.

follow-up letter	determination	hardware	software
clients	genius	installed	senior

21. parts of a computer system _____

22. someone in the fourth year
    of high school or college _____

23. program of commands that directs a computer

    _____

24. a person with extraordinary intelligence _____

25. set in place for use or service _____

26. people who use the services of a company _____

27. habit of following through on decisions _____

28. formal letter sent to a company _____

Directions: On the lines below, write a word from the list to finish each sentence.

abroad	government	politician
advantages	gymnasium	instinct

29. The team met in the school's _____.

30. Juan will spend the summer _____ in France.

31. What do you know about the _____ of your town?

32. At the sound of thunder, some dogs follow their
    _____ and hide.

33. There are many _____ to knowing how to use a computer.

34. Theodore Roosevelt was a famous _____.

Part D

Think About the Stories

Who Did What?

◆ **Directions:** Answer each question with the name of a person from the stories in Chapter 3.

Paul	**Bill Gates**	**Mr. Lee**
Mae	**Teddy Roosevelt**	**Jen**

1. Who owns a store in the East Mall? _____

2. Who left college to start a computer software business? _____

3. Who could not go camping due to illness? _____

4. Who wrote a follow-up business letter to a storeowner? _____

5. Who helped others learn how to play soccer? _____

6. Who was very sick as a child? _____

Why Did It Happen?

◆ **Directions:** Draw a line from each event in Column A to its effect in Column B.

Column A	**Column B**
7. Because he loved animals,	○ the girls made sure the campfire was out.
8. Since forest fires harm animals and their homes,	○ Bill Gates is the richest man in the world.
9. Since female cicadas lay their eggs in branches,	○ Paul followed a strict schedule.
10. Because millions of people buy his computer software,	○ Teddy Roosevelt could not shoot the bear cub.
11. Since he needed to be at work on time,	○ Mae was a volunteer soccer coach.
12. Because her school started a community service program,	○ the adults mate in treetops.

Where Did It Happen?

◆ **Directions:** This list has the names of some places where stories took place. Write each place name next to the story it goes with.

the woods   a school auditorium   a shopping mall

13. "Learning Curve," Parts 1 and 2 _____

14. "We're Not Alone" _____

15. "A Talent to Lead" _____

Chapter 1 Story Words

◆ **Directions:** Write the words from the Story Words section of each lesson.

LESSON 1 ▶ **Flip Flop: A Fine Dog, Part 1**

_____

_____

_____

_____

_____

LESSON 2 ▶ **Flip Flop: A Fine Dog, Part 2**

_____

_____

_____

_____

_____

LESSON 3 ▶ **Into the Eye**

_____

_____

_____

_____

_____

Chapter 1 Story Words, continued

LESSON 4   ▶ **John Muir: The Father of Our National Parks**

_____

_____

_____

_____

_____

LESSON 5   ▶ **Dear Journal**

_____

_____

_____

_____

_____

LESSON 6   ▶ **Devil Down Under**

_____

_____

_____

_____

_____

Chapter 1 Story Words, continued

LESSON 7 ▶ **Making a Difference: Airline Ambassadors**

_____

_____

_____

_____

_____

_____

Chapter 2 Story Words

◆ **Directions:** Write the words from the Story Words section of each lesson.

LESSON 1 ▶ **Double Trouble, Part 1**

_____

_____

_____

_____

_____

_____

LESSON 2 ▶ **Double Trouble, Part 2**

_____

_____

_____

_____

_____

LESSON 3 ▶ **Book Talk**

_____

_____

_____

_____

_____

_____

Chapter 2 Story Words, continued

LESSON 4 ▶ **Out of This World Research, Part 1**

_____

_____

_____

_____

_____

_____

LESSON 5 ▶ **Out of This World Research, Part 2**

_____

_____

_____

_____

_____

_____

LESSON 6 ▶ **Slam Dunk**

_____

_____

_____

_____

_____

_____

Chapter 2 Story Words, continued

LESSON 7 ▶ As Far As the Eye Can See

_____

_____

_____

_____

_____

_____

Chapter 3 Story Words

◆ **Directions:** Write the words from the Story Words section of each lesson.

LESSON 1   ▶ **Learning Curve, Part 1**

_____

_____

_____

_____

LESSON 2   ▶ **Learning Curve, Part 2**

_____

_____

_____

_____

LESSON 3   ▶ **We're Not Alone**

_____

_____

_____

WORD BANK

Chapter 3 Story Words, continued

LESSON 4   ▶ **Cicada Cycle**

_____

_____

_____

_____

_____

LESSON 5   ▶ **A Talent to Lead**

_____

_____

_____

_____

_____

LESSON 6   ▶ **A Man Ahead of His Time**

_____

_____

_____

_____

_____

WORD BANK

Chapter 3 Story Words, continued

LESSON 7 ▶ Teddy's Bear

_____

_____

_____

_____

_____

Notes